T0039211

Swimming in Cosmic Soup

Second Edition

Philosophical and Physics Musings on Life in the Twenty-First Century

Russ Otter

SWIMMING IN COSMIC SOUP
Philosophical and Physics Musings on Life in the Twenty-First Century

iUniverse books may be ordered through booksellers or by contacting:

iUniverse
1663 Liberty Drive
Bloomington, IN 47403
www.iuniverse.com
1-800-Authors (1-800-288-4677)

ISBN: 978-1-4917-1860-5 (sc)
ISBN: 978-1-4917-1862-9 (hc)
ISBN: 978-1-4917-1861-2 (e)

Library of Congress Control Number: 2013923263

Print information available on the last page.

iUniverse rev. date: 10/15/2015

To my family, and deeply in honor of my mother, Doris Otter.

Who was the personification of the Golden Rule through her common sense, humor, and love for everyone.

Is your Cosmic Soup Swim Sentimental or Kind?

Contents

ACKNOWLEDGMENTS

Thanks to Robin Smith for her invaluable editorial assistance with my original treatise draft in 2006. However, the literary style is to be blamed on myself alone. Thanks also to Randy Dilday Sr., Jim Dilday, Vicki Otter, Stan and Mary Tomlinson, and Bennett Tsou for their contributions in reviewing my early treatise. Also, a special thanks to author Rev. Paul Peck for his very early review and encouragement.

Thanks again to Jim Dilday for his current editorial review and advice with my Second Edition.

And a most special thank-you to my friend and renowned author and artist Don Kracke, for without his encouragement, this second edition might not exist.

Much of the artwork is from unknown artists, with the exception of Don Kracke and Vicki Otter, and I deeply thank them all for their adept works of beauty and talent.

PURPOSE

This book is a wonderful journey, compelling, thought-provoking, and balanced in the end. I hope you agree and enjoy the wonder of knowledge, mystery, and thinking we are all built upon, for that is my legacy's objective: to take life with all its paragons-perfections and beauty coupled with heinous horrors, while telling the truth from an objective point of view.

Of course, realize that we need to navigate the treachery fraught with bias that often poisons true knowledge within our finite *sentient beings*. We are still eons away from greater truths and eventually less bias and greater acceptance of life's truths. My objective is to express fact simply and well; however, some may argue about my science and philosophy, to be sure. Still, the paramount core of the events and scope of the essays and ultimate story in the end is to build candor among us without dismantling our humanity and to open our mind's eyes. That is the beauty of this book, I believe; it takes truths from the traditions we have learned from and couples them with our most recent knowledge, which is expanding and coalescing the real truths of those early foundations daily. I simply ask and hope you review this book with an open mind.

This book's true agenda is not for self-gain alone but for unity, not for sentiment but for kindness, not for competition but for cooperation.

We have come far, and farther still goes our path. One way to look at this book, tethered to its art, is as an awesome journey we take together. I believe this journey can possibly be unsettling, but I also believe it will be exciting and beautiful. As we improve our knowledge, we improve the world and the equities that entails. To paraphrase Socrates: "Knowledge is goodness. Lack of knowledge is evil."

Sincerely, Russ

Postscript: This book is divided into two books. The first is the cycle of life from the beginning of our universe through to where we are today. The second half is where we are headed tomorrow; it is more a collection of essays based on science as I view it, and it is a sometimes inscrutable ride. I hope you find it an engaging ride through philosophy, history, and science as it questions assumptions and the great unknowns.

Finally, I hope you enjoy both the art and the rhetoric of mystery, discovery, and hope!

Time Will Tell

I believe that what I have written is true; it is how I have come to understand life. I actually may be in error and fully off my rickety rocker. Certainly I do not understand everything within our cosmic soup—this infinite abyss we call our home.

What I do believe is that we all are part of the same reality, the same universe, and the same family—yesterday, today, and tomorrow. I believe that good is immutable and void of superstition and mythology. However, I believe humanity has so greatly succumbed to superstitions and mythology that the immutable nature of good has been misrepresented and dismantled.

With goodness dismantled by way of misinformation, knowledge and truth have partially become vacuums filled with chaos, and the selfish ease of convenience, thus given over to suppositions without challenge or reason. This lack of real knowledge is the prime reason for many of the human-made evils (wars, carnage, selfishness, and horror) present in our world. Time will continue to tell the truth as we mature with knowledge.

Perhaps someday, no doubt centuries from now, we will realize that the human race, as well as all life, is valuable, interdependent, and inexorably connected. With that deeper knowledge, we may mature, letting go of selfishness and fear that arise out of mythology, superstition, and ego; put down our swords; and begin to live with greater peace and decency.

INTRODUCTION

Our cosmic soup is in endless churn, changing the circumstances of events moment to moment. This constant movement and change require us to use reason, and understand circumstances, before judgment. The *swim meet* is on every moment someone chooses to join in, to mature and to grow. However, ideologues will require a few swimming lessons.

Sometimes and Sometimes was the title I almost used for this book. It seemed an appropriate title as well, as life is an equation buffet ad infinitum. The nuances and varieties of unique situations abound and confound the senses, making it difficult to make the right choices. I swim in this cosmic soup every waking moment to discover, learn, fail, and grow. This ethereal swim has been present from my youth until this current day as I continue to try to understand life. It has always seemed that the answers to questions and how to behave have evolved as a *sometimes and sometimes* proposition.

Circumstances Matter, It's That Simple

Certainly if I had been born at the other end of the block or community, or run into a different set of friends, or lost a parent through divorce and ended up with a different set of parents, and so forth, would I not have been a different person? Or if not totally different, would I have been exposed to values and experiences that would have substantially altered my experiences and consequently shaped my views of life, putting me in an altered state from where I sit today?

My answer is yes to some extent, and perhaps substantially. However, I will never really know.

What I do know is that my life was substantially shaped in my adolescence, a time when I began to really question the meaning of infinity, of life within that context, and what our place within this universe and this life actually means.

The thought-provoking experiences I had as an adolescent led me to question, even more closely, what was real and true. What was the *common denominator*, as I used to call it (and still do), that ties all of humanity together in an immutable and irrefutable form? The luxury of illusion was assailed by my deepest senses, which measured the value and clarity of my thinking. If I had not found the universal answer—*that truth must be for all people, or it is not truth*—these deep senses, this internalized focused trepidation and wonder from the unknown depths of infinity and of what and where we are in this universe, would have slayed any false premises I tried to hold onto. Hence, the search for the common denominator of life began in earnest. My mental state had found its own integrity and would not allow me to fake this journey.

Religion played a role early on as I searched for answers to what life was within this infinite realm. However, that road faded away through a somewhat protracted epiphany after some religious involvement and much review. It had become clear that organized religion, with its very human origins, lacked in my search for truth—that search for the common denominator whereby all of humanity is humanely and fairly measured within its foundations.

Furthermore, the scholarship used to compile centuries-old references regarding the gods or a God and their ancient representatives is robust with discrepancies. In our modern era, we simply do not have credible evidence for the foundations we have based much of our civilization's religious beliefs and behaviors upon. The majority of theological scholars will admit that the New Testament has more discrepancies between the original Greek and Latin manuscripts than there are words in the New Testament. Some of the verses and stories in our current gospels never appeared in the original Greek scriptural manuscripts. They may have been added as folklore or due to theological bias, or possibly added later on for ease of reading purposes. Certainly the history of the development of the King James, or standard, version of the Bible has been a centuries-long political and theological struggle to consolidate ultimately competing personal views of who and what God and Jesus are.

Therefore, as you read this book, you will understand why I devoted so much of it in chapters four, five, and six to theocracy and religion, as the foundations of all religions, including the Quran, are at the very core of our cultural civilizations. The ancient religions of our world underpin modern-day life, and they are an important subject that warrants greater personal review by all of us.

Many religions illustrate some critically sound fundamental principles that, at their heart, concentrate on the soundest of ethics and cultural foundations born of the Golden Rule. This principle is at the very core of what is universally decent and valuable to individuals and societies. However, almost everything else in many of these religious texts is weighted toward supposition, based on the clergy's pulpit opinions and translated by early authors, scribes, and monks, each with a distinct mission. Not all of these are bad by any means, but they are not all the essence of a decent religious life or what I would describe as ethical teachings, which could or should have been the ultimate potential from religion.

You will find some sound scholarship regarding religions, primarily Judeo-Christian, in reviewing some engaging books written by the chair of Religious Studies at North Carolina University, Chapel Hill. The author's name is Bart Ehrman, a scholar of the first order. Bart Ehrman took a long road to find out for himself the truth about the words written in the Judeo-Christian Bible. He learned Greek, Hebrew, and Latin to research the original manuscripts of the Old and New Testaments. Much of what is in the commonly used standard Bible, first printed, not written by hand, in the fifteenth century, is not altogether accurate. On this point, most theological scholars, I believe, would agree. As Bart Ehrman points out, the Bible is not the inerrant word of God, as he had once believed.

I personally believe the Bible is a book fraught with inadvertent copy errors, as well as some well-intended and theologically motivated textual changes, causing the Bible as it has been sorted and edited throughout the ages to be a worldly book of human beliefs, impressions, and persuasions, far less than a sacrosanct divine document. Without question, the necessary rigors of translating ancient stories to preserve their accuracy is lacking in our ancient scriptural manuscripts. Additionally, the New Testament today is based on one particular sect of early Christianity that won out over several other sects that competed in the early centuries of Christianity. These competing Christian sects had conflicting visions of who Jesus was and what he believed, as well as who and what God or the gods were.

As a starting point in reviewing the history of the New Testament, I would recommend reading *Misquoting Jesus* by Bart Ehrman, which addresses these questions in a scholarly and serious manner.

Swimming in Cosmic Soup is my perspective as a layperson regarding subject matter that is at the core of our species. I hope it shows respect for everyone, regardless of your agreement or disagreement with me. I could be any of you if born under your circumstances, and you could be me. That is a principle that is always in the forefront of my consciousness when I am doing my best in this life. My perspectives are based on some scholarly study, but primarily reflect my personal understanding regarding the general, scientific, political, religious, and cultural makeup of our world.

My strongest influences in life came from my own conscious mental math as to what is good and what is not, with reinforcement and enlightenment coming from the wit, wisdom, humor, and scholarly efforts of others too numerous to mention.

This book collates those personal and assimilated bits of knowledge.

Again, I almost called this book *Sometimes and Sometimes* because I find human beings or sentient beings at their highest functioning level rely on judgment, on discretion, on this thing called understanding, which finds justice in sometimes forgiveness and sometimes consequences.

This capability to use nuanced qualitative judgment makes us actually human, rather than rule-based amoebas or robots. In all things, I believe we should see situations/issues/questions as a *sometimes and a sometimes* decision or judgment based on circumstance.

This exploitation of sound judgment is one of the highest values humanity places upon us.

I hope the call to use measured judgments in lieu of ideological or strictly rule-based actions comes across clearly in this book.

To put this into different and concise words, I would simply say: to achieve justice takes more than the rule of law or separatist doctrines; it takes a sense of humanity and understanding to execute mature and fair human judgment.

One of the problems encountered when making judgments involves one of our primary communication tools: our language. Words can play havoc much too often. Words are sometimes used rhetorically, both intentionally and unintentionally, to skew, deflect, make ambiguous, and obscure the subject at hand. Words afford various interpretations and are sometimes used to specifically obfuscate, coupled with the fact that words are only a means to convey a concept; they are not the concept, and so lack some dimension or perspective. Only personal human judgment and open communication that avoids personally vested emotion are capable of grasping the full intent or meaning of thought.

I raise the issue of *personal emotion* within communication because once personal emotion is released into the arena of communication, effective or proper respect for the subject can become lost. In such emotional situations, respect for developing one's knowledge and understanding regarding the subject becomes secondary as personal egos become the focus of such emotion-based communication. Therefore, only more strident opponents are developed, not effective communication or knowledge.

It takes respect for your opponent, however much considered a scoundrel or ignoramus, to ameliorate or to win over. Logic does not succeed within personal emotion or arrogance, but within a humility that respects all life, be it good or bad. Paradoxically, the truth is that without opposites in life, nothing exists. In other words, we need darkness in order to have light, without unhappiness we would not have happiness, without sorrow we could not know joy, without evil we do not have goodness. Opposites are an *infinite absolute,* hence a conundrum that should humble us all into the respecting and loving of all things in our quest for doing well by ourselves and for others, even for those with whom we vehemently disagree.

Respect for your opponent requires wisdom, humility, and courage.

Courage has many intrinsic virtues, but none more than when courage disciplines emotions into repose, and in so doing, allows honesty to fully breathe, even when it disembowels our own previous notions of sacrosanct truth or requires us to quiet indignation's volatile will.

All great leaders have known this truth and practiced it—Jesus, Gandhi, Martin Luther King, the Dalai Lama, and others—but the list is far too short.

In summary, this book contains multiple subjects, all linked by physical and psychological boundaries. They are the subjects of science, politics, religion, cultural behaviors, leadership, humor, and the physical universe we live within: *our cosmic soup.* The chapters begin with the foundation of life, our universe, and then progress through the pillars upon pillars, that established our religious and cultural foundations, coupled with the politics and results we live with today.

I began writing this manuscript to document my questions and answers about life; and to further examine the value of good and the importance of knowledge and integrity and what they really are, as well as where we are today.

In this second edition, I have added some additional essays, primarily on science, but also as well on our review of the cycle of life we all are embodied in together.

I measure life against a humane constant rather than fair-weather culture, religion, or politics. That constant is the Golden Rule. I use the Golden Rule in this book as the key benchmark by which I measure how the ages have manifested themselves.

The following topics are highlighted in this book:

- a review of the scientific knowledge we have of our universe in brief and simple-to-understand terms and what that might mean to us
- a look at religion from a perspective that I have not heard addressed, one for which all sentient people everywhere are equally capable of engaging in the fruits of (It is perhaps the pure and simple meaning of a loving religious life, whose teachings are removed from the human extrapolations, rituals, suppositions, and institutions put into place in the last few thousand years by humankind.)
- a pragmatic view of theocratic histories and the fallout we are living with today as a result

- an examination of the politically correct, for which I leave no stone unturned for the mischief these folks have wrought on society (This book presents an approach to responsibility, freedom, and ethics from a point of common sense, rather than from a fixed point of law.)

- a look at the nature of politics and the direction of my own politics, coupled with the ultimate force and value of humor

- a more complex review of physics/science/philosophy and the unknowns that play with our mysteries, dreams, and hopes, through the lens of the great work that philosophers, scientists, and physicists are doing moment by moment to improve our lives by examining humanity's cultures and values and by revealing new scientific possibilities and truths

- my journey for values, not out of any moral duty, but a journey born of a necessity to find some bit of understanding, truth, and peace within my life

The only good is knowledge, and the only evil is ignorance.
—Socrates

Part I

Chapter 1

UNIVERSE

Only two things are infinite, the universe and human stupidity, and I'm not sure about the former.
—Albert Einstein

Here we begin with the most basic of cosmic realities: the unknowable realm of the universe and infinity. Thus begins our journey through the cosmic soup, and a good day for a swim!

Our universe is a physical reality, which evolves. The universe consists of *matter* and *energy*. Beyond that, *we* also know with relative certainty, short of an anomaly here or there, that it will eventually give itself over to a *closed universe* or an *open universe* conclusion. Beyond that, it is open for debate and study.

If it is a closed universe, then at some point, the matter (stars, planets, and galaxies) will stop expanding and begin to contract back to the big crunch. In a closed universe that collapses back on itself, the atoms will actually break down and cease to exist from the unbounded extremes of heat generated through growing velocities and densities. This may very well be our current universe's end, and then perhaps we will have another big bang. No one knows.

The other scenario, which has become the most likely end result given our new understandings of the universe, is that we live in an open universe that will continue to expand and accelerate, and eventually all of the energy will exhaust itself. Our own sun will burn out, as will all other suns, and all other energy sources in our universe will die out as well—leaving our universe's end to one of perhaps pure darkness and absolute cold. Still, remember that those anomalies I spoke of can possibly change the playing field of our irascible physics at any time.

In any event, we are evolving with a physical set of cosmic laws; one might call them God's laws. We currently have no manner in which to alter these, our physical realities. This is the universe we live in. It is that simple. However, for the purposes of our emotional lives, we are not really impacted by these physical consequences, save our own sense of finality about the universe and how that knowledge might alter our choices in life. Certainly, if we ever had advance knowledge of a catastrophic asteroid impacting the earth, our cosmic-soup swimming styles would flux and change a bit, I would imagine.

From my perspective, the universe I am speaking of is only the one we exist in. You might call it the universe with a lower case "u" versus the *infinite reality* that there is actually a Universe with a capital "U," which involves infinity beyond the confines of the Big-Bang bubble we have come to know as our universe. One other aspect of our universe is the largely unknown, undefined, not fully understood, or as Einstein defined it, the spooky realm of quantum physics. Specifically Einstein was referring to the aspects of "entanglement," which I will discuss in a moment.

Quantum physics is the world of atomic-sized and subatomic-sized particles that are the building blocks that make up all matter of objects—such as people, cars, concrete, plastic, food, planets, and stars, in other words, all of the objects we touch, see, and interact with. The quantum world of molecules, atoms, electrons, and quarks is the building blocks of matter. The micro-quantum world does not behave as our larger macro world of matter does. It defies all common sense and all logic as we understand those terms today. For example, if I throw a baseball at a wall with two windows, it will pass through one of the windows. But in the quantum world, if you project (throw) an electron or photon at two windows on a wall, it will pass through both windows at the same time. *See,* it makes no sense within our current understanding of physics from within our macro world, but it proves out by experiment within the micro-world of quantum mechanics. Even more intriguing is the aspect of *entanglement*, the process of two entangled particles, which may be millions of miles apart, but when one particle has its state of spin or polarity changed, the other entangled particle, millions of miles away, will change its state at the same time. These separated particles communicate with each other as if they were one object.

Truly the universe, the nature of life, and existence itself are wonders beyond our natural senses. By examination and experimentation, with further time, we will perhaps only marvel at their wonder the closer we come to finding any real understanding of their nature; but it is clear that while there is much we do not yet understand, our journey toward understanding our universe in just the last few decades has traveled exponentially farther than at any previous time in history.

Consequently in the twenty-first century, we have come to understand more about our universe than our predecessors. Individuals today have more information upon which to base their decisions; to know what is true and what is left unknown; to know how to behave and think; as well as to know why thinking critically and behaving well should be important.

Individuals in the twenty-first century should be less influenced by mythology and superstitions and should be able to abide by their integrity, their personal relationship with ethics, with good, and with their personal definition and relationship with a possible God. Human beings have always had the ability to choose right and wrong and to think for themselves, but it was far more clouded and impeded by superstition and myth in times past. In the world today, we have the lessons of history, the knowledge of greater science, and our personal integrity all working together in choosing an ethical and logical life—or not.

I hope our choices are essentially premised on the here and now. I hope that we have faith in the value of doing good and then do it, as some great and wise leaders throughout history have told us to do.

Life is a spectrum of positive and negative, good and bad, kindness and cruelty, love and hate. Will you choose the positive forms of actions in life, as the results not only benefit you, but others at the same time? Everyone wins. Inversely, to operate in the negative manner, you may well enhance your own life with wealth and pleasure, but at the expense of others. One system of behavior wins for all people, and the other system wins for only a portion of the people.

This is the simple essence of existence within our universe.

Therefore, truth within this universe, for me, is based on a personal and very pragmatic relationship with yourself. One could say with your god, in a sense.

As we make our behavioral decisions, we also know that time and space are our physical home, our cosmic mousetrap, if you will, from which we shall not escape. However, since a universe by definition is infinite, there is nowhere to escape to! Therefore, our universe becomes more than just a physical aspect; it also contains our awareness, our sense of being, our personal universe, as well as our physical. It is the marriage of these two realms that can confound us, unite us, and divide us in our daily pursuit for purpose and truth and, most importantly, in how we behave.

It's that simple for me. I do not mean to say that it is easy, because it is often maddening attempting to deal with the awing nature of the unrelenting unknown. But it is that simple.

We are in search of our universe, both physical and personal, and that quest has done much to misguide us, horrify us, harm us, inform us, and love us. And it will continue to do so. The choice of the manner in which we take this journey is ours.

Let us hope we improve as stewards in this quest.

Chapter 2

SUPPOSE

Impossibilities allow us the possible.

Suppose infinity has no external point, just as Isaac Newton supposed of space. Well, that is the reality we live about, in, and of. To assert otherwise is to assert ignorance within its fullness of myopic glory! In the same way, it could be argued time has no external point, even though the future, some would argue, is the external point, as it has not happened. I seek to improve on that explanation in this essay, as well as confirm the implicit union of space and time, which exists within the non-restrictive expression of infinity.

Hence, space, time, and infinity are in super-union and never will disengage, save the fact that they both exist and do not exist by way of their omniscience.

That is a conundrum that by reading other chapters in part 2 of this book, the subject matter here may be better understood.

In part 2 of this book, I discuss these essential summaries of ideas in a more specific manner: from energy improvement, which links well to my thoughts on values and even the issue of a chapter titled "Everything Is Nothing, and Nothing Is Everything." I hope you have a chance to review my struggling efforts to express these endless issues and in so doing find that they augment this important discussion between science and philosophy and the sound hopes they portend.

But likely not! Life is a conundrum, to be certain.

Once we understand the scope of life's reality, we grasp a form of metaphysics that runs this show we call existence. Although metaphysics is not an excuse to avoid what cannot be explained, it is a richer understanding of the fact that humility is the key to success in this life and that understanding that key opens doors of knowledge that cannot be found by any other means. But please try to enjoy the journey of discovery, of hope, and of mystery.

To further explain this convoluted paradox of life's realities, let's begin where we opened this chapter:

Just as space has always been and always will be, so is time.

To illustrate this:

Understand that it takes time, the same infinite expanse of time, to reach the infinite so-called corners of space. *Note: Space has no corners, save within the possible notion of multidimensional spaces, which in fact are not really corners, as they are overlaid by general space. This is true of our simple three-dimensional spaces. These corners, if you will, are used to delineate functions, operational means of measurements, but they are artificial lines on an infinite canvas of both space and time.*

In other words, if you have space, you must have the time to reach the endless bounds of space, which equates time as a boundless nature without an external point, just as Isaac Newton pointed out about space.

The future events that will come with time are only events that occur on time's infinite pre-endowed canvas.

This always has been and always will be. It is called simply infinity. The superunion of time and space equals the irascible and simple infinity—forever and a day.

Yet time and space, as well as infinity, and let's throw in perhaps gravity, since particle physics still has yet to identify the graviton, the elementary particle missing to better complete the theory of particle physics. The graviton may or may not exist within the finite bubble we call our universe, the big bang, therefore changing our fundamental understanding of physics. Keep in mind that gravity itself may be infinite rather than finite, as the elements of particle physics define the finite only. Remember that beyond our big bang, there is an emptiness called space that may hold trillions upon trillions or rather infinite numbered objects that we call big bangs. But it also holds the existence of what we cannot define, as we have no access.

Infinity, along with time and space, are infinite, which mathematically defies explanation, as you cannot define what is infinite. If you could define what is infinite, it would be circumscribed, that is, it would become finite.

This conclusive evidence that we are part of the *impossibility* called infinity, which we have no capacity to fully define, gives us the *possibility* of our finite existence. And within this finite realm, we are forever given the means to discover and discover and discover anew. This is science's most glorious journey.

Let's suppose, as I have said, that the space that lies beyond our own big bang is made up from elementary particles, some of which we may or may not know of today. That is all we can know, besides the implicit fact that our big bang is expanding into this vacant space, not necessarily because of dark matter or dark energy, but by the simple math of particle physics' continuous manufacturing of more and more elementary particles, as we can observe via the Large Hadron Collider (LHC), near Geneva, Switzerland, and other particle colliders. In other words, perhaps the reason gravity is losing to the expansion of space, or to what we call dark matter and dark energy pulling us apart, is altogether different. Or suppose it is one and the same?

Just suppose . . .

We are expanding like a river, overflowing its banks, due to the constant generation of elementary particles forcing us to exceed our shores. As such, gravity's strengths are reduced, save at our event horizons and black holes.

Just suppose . . .

Yet we seem to be gripped in a myopic state of believing that we will have the aptitude to understand what it is not possible to know.

First we must understand that principle, and then our seemingly impossible position of not having the complete capacity to understand actually provides us, as I said before, with the possibility to discover forever, with the endgame being a better life and world for all. Science is the ultimate equalizer, the ultimate equity, that dethrones demagogues, invented knowledge, superstitions, myths, and the selfish, therefore forcing us to accept our equal betterment.

Science can do this, for example by discovering ubiquitous energy, which will unite the world in a more common and fairer playing field. It will do this someday, and communication and treatment of others will only improve.

Suppose that Albert Einstein, Isaac Newton, and Niels Bohr did not have all of the answers correct. They knew they had some right and were guessing with hope and wisdom for the others, but they never understood, save by way of philosophy, the bigger picture that physicists and scientists understand more and more today with our more recent empirical scientific discoveries. Those discoveries, such as entanglements and superpositions and the expansion of the universe, were denied them in many experimental manners. These recent new discoveries, along with our reaches into *string theory* and other possibilities to unify the universe and its makeup, have given us more data to review. This new data should also philosophically and scientifically be drawing us closer to the bigger picture that impossibilities allow our possibilities to be sentient and discover, and that the principle that we are limited sentient beings in terms of understanding infinity should be paramount.

There are still many who believe that our big bang is the whole universe. It certainly is not. It is a pixel on the big screen of infinity. We, therefore, are, as I have written before, universally a part of *everything* and *nothing* (see chapter 32) at the same time and in the same space. As these terms are fortunately not definable, as they are impossible to define, ironically this gives us our very breaths.

Note: *Entanglement is when two protons or perhaps photons entangle and separate in space and can be millions of miles or billions of miles apart, but when one entangled elementary particle is impacted or changed by way of polarity, or spin, the other particle billions of miles away changes at the same time. This violates the speed of light as it applies to communication.*

Einstein thought there were so-called mathematical hidden-variables to make entanglement possible. In my view, he was right and wrong. In conventional terms or finite terms, there are no hidden variables; that is what the mystery and bridge entanglement show us about the nature of infinity.

Infinity is not possible mathematically as it has no beginning nor end, no start time nor end time, yet it is still our foundation from which we exist within our finite state of existence with beginnings and endings, with alphas and omegas.

My point is that *there is neither time nor space, and yet there is all time and all space forever.* This impossible superposition allows us to exist in the finite and from within our roots of the infinite all at one time and in one space. We truly are *one.* To exist in the infinite per se, you could not have identity, ego, knowledge, hope, joy, or pain, all of which are limiting by finite definition and hence are finite and violate being infinite.

This is where philosophy and science merge and need to improve their true sentient tether. Science and philosophy need to merge more effectively to advance science and philosophy, to impact our perspectives, and to better open our minds' eyes. The great majority of us are currently so far away from our end hopes and dreams. For example, for every one child that smiles in the world, five others are crying in squalor. We all need to improve on that as a world community. The more we understand the melding of science and philosophy, we will grow for the better; otherwise we will continue to limit our growth, thus slowing down the building of our essential true knowledge to better our humanity.

Education is critical, and improved knowledge is critical to all of our hopes and dreams.

It is within sentient wisdom, or philosophy, along with the intricacies of science, that we will find the truth and better ourselves and others. That is the goal we have long been guiding ourselves toward, whether we are aware of it or not.

I believe this type of communication should be of greater discussion, and believe it will ultimately better us—in our humanity, our humor, our goodwill toward others, and the best of our healthy hopes for all of us.

Chapter 3

VANITY OF VANITIES

Clichés so often befall vain people.
—Ann Beattie

"*Vanity of vanities; all is vanity*," so said Solomon in the book of Ecclesiastics—and Solomon is held up in the Judeo-Christian religious tradition to be the wisest man who ever lived.

Understanding history gives us much to leverage our knowledge building, but it does not, nor can it, change our universal future. That future is substantially predestined by science, by the universe's grasp of its own physics of our future, both as mere objects of *matter and energy* as well as living sentient forms *of matter and energy*. And our future is not forever, as some may believe. It is inevitably based on what Joseph Campbell, the renowned mythologist, author, and lecturer, once said, that in the big picture of existence (and I paraphrase), "Nothing matters." In other words, all of our current, future, and historical works toward understanding, toward the arts, the Beethovens and Michelangelos of the world, come to nothing once time casts its final curtain on our specific big-bang's final existence.

In my view, Joseph Campbell mirrors the *wisdom of Solomon*. So if this is true, what does it mean? What is the point?

To be specific about the phrase "Nothing matters," or rather, to put it into context, I would say that the moment is all that we have that does matter, but beyond our current *relative moments*, hence, *the here and now*, we are captives of a greater play, which cannot be rewritten. All of our achievements, our long-term understandings, will pass away into the abyss of the non-existent—someday.

So it is important to understand that the here and now, the moment for which we live, is plain and simply *everything* and that the moment matters. Our conduct, our caring, our continued expansion of knowledge are important in the here and now. Knowledge and the shoulders we have been held up by from our history give us the means to ameliorate hardship and improve on life and our caring for others less fortunate.

That is what matters.

Only the knowledge we can obtain in the here and now and then execute upon it is of any real importance or permanence. An example would be our commitment to stem-cell or cancer research or understanding the evolution of life and death from cultures and species both past and present and the ultimate reach toward where we came from and where we are ultimately heading, hence, our cosmological and physical world.

So, as nothing matters in the larger scheme of life, everything matters in this relative moment of life. And we should embrace it with the wisdom of the ages, with that knowledge of our predecessors' experiences and artistic fulfillment, which makes us better and wiser.

To believe in the fullness of reality, which will forever be an unknown, should be reclassified as a simple belief in *the science of knowledge*, the *science of knowledge* as it has been handed to us through the struggles of the ages. The heroic heretics, such as the Galileos, gave us the integrity and logic to believe in more than mere myth and superstition.

We should not be arguing in this life about the reason we are here, as that is an unknowable. We should be arguing on how to make all lives better by way of our improved knowledge of the cosmos and our reading of history. I would argue that improving that knowledge comes from lifting standards and progressing toward genuine peace.

As Socrates said, "The only good is knowledge, and the only evil is ignorance."

I believe Socrates had it right, just as the continual ebb and flow of the knowledge we have obtained from science has held Socrates to be correct.

What a world we would have if we could reduce our arguments to what matters (what we know), not to opinion or wishful suppositions . . . just imagine!

Knowledge, life, and existence ultimately belong to vanity's abyss, as Solomon intimated very directly and I would argue as well—as Joseph Campbell wisely reasoned.

So what is the moral of this paradox, this infinite conundrum as some may see it, this story I am trying to tell.

It is that all we have and know are mere tools for good or bad, and are best used as gifts of good, by way of humility, regardless of what matters from our history or our futures. History and the future are our benefactors, providing us with knowledge in the moment; they are not important in and of themselves. In other words, what matters is the here and now.

So find a way to *enjoy life.*

There is gold at the bottom of every endeavor, even in failure,

As you truly know what you have at the bottom: nothing.

And Appreciation fares a lot, in other words, appreciation is the real gold in life.

This is where values travail in the *moment* of taking account of what we have to offer and to make our time provide something better for others. And in that moment, for ourselves as well.

Everything is the same under the sun yesterday, today, and tomorrow. But all that matters is today, as yesterday and tomorrow so wisely continue to teach us.

All other issues are temporal to the moment, even though paradoxically all moments are by definition temporal. This paradox is the glue of life itself. [1]

This is the core point of genuine virtue, of humility, of goodness.

If the potentates of this world, secular and religious, operated by this fundamental holy and cosmic truth for which they actually blindly teach, we would be better off. But for pride and tribal mentalities, it falls on deaf ears, and therefore many of our historic and current leaders more often contribute to warring rhetoric, and thereby often make all living things far less better off, and the ironies of life continue to multiply, derailing our simple truths.

At any rate, *appreciate the moment* with a respect for others, and you will do all you can to improve this world and yourself. Nothing more or less is required. That is the essence of the Golden Rule. [2]

[1] See chapter 32, "Everything Is Nothing, and Nothing Is Everything.".

[2] See chapter 15, "It Only Takes One Thing."

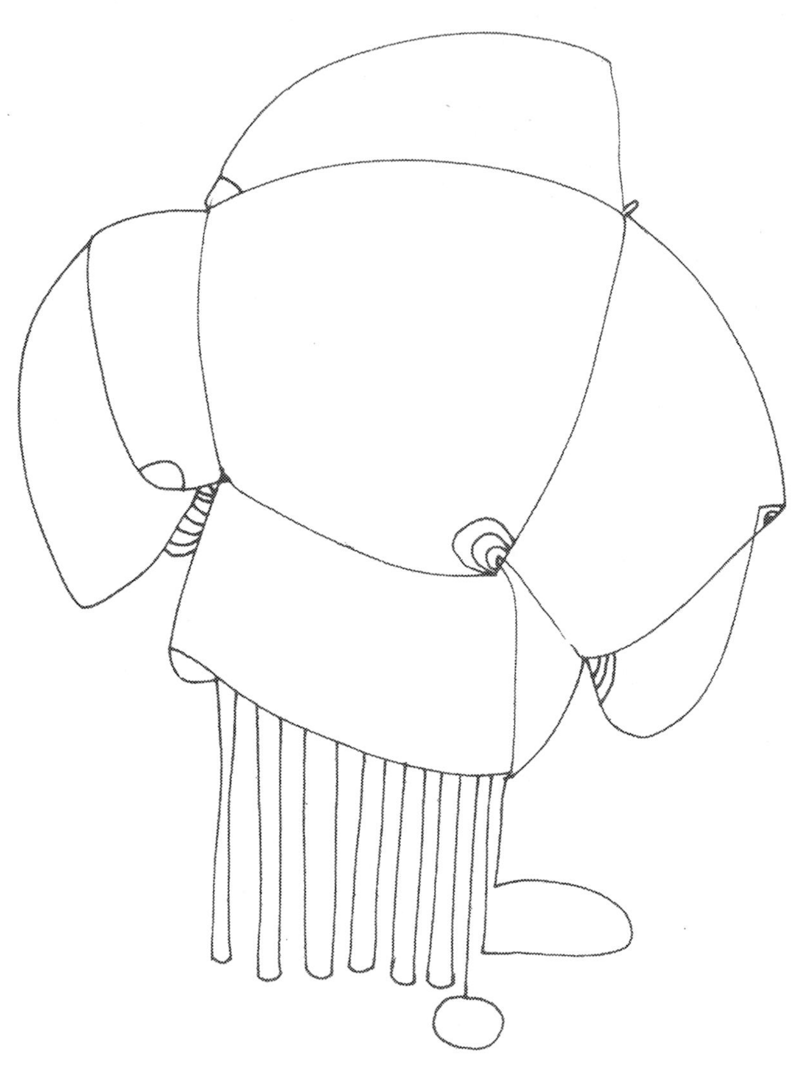

Chapter 4

THEOCRACY

If God did not exist, it would be necessary to invent him.
—Voltaire

Theocracy *is* a political body or state governed by an invisible deity through the medium of the prophets or by officials thought to be divinely guided. A belief in a government by divine guidance.

Theocracies, in general, are by history's record cruel, if not the cruelest form of government in their torture of humanity. Just review your history:

Theocracies are generally based on unchecked dogma, disguised as moral foundations.

Can one think of a more unreasoned position to guide actions than theocracy?

To rely on faith as a leader is the abandonment of reason, the voiding of morality incarnate.

No fundamental theocratic government should be allowed to run any nation *if it aspires in doctrine* to kill others of other faiths or enslave and deny people individual opportunity.

Faith in theocracy conjures positions unrelenting, intractable, and fully corruptible, which allows reason no place at its table.

Secular despots of the cruelest natures measure equal to theocratic institutions, both of which deny freedom and lack moral ethos.

I fear theocracy is the cruelest enemy of humankind, even of Providence itself. For Providence, if actual, would by definition be the very face of natural truths, a vestal virgin of evidence, soiled only by unreasoned mythological and superstitious minds.

Certainly Europe and America have built the modern world out of the ruins of such theocratic histories and have wisely attempted to form governing bodies that are shielded from theocratic institutions.

Still, the shoulders of history's less knowledgeable times, the inner search for meaning in humankind's early development, hold us hostage today. For the mythological cornerstones of our origins have never been examined by the fundamentals of reason with sufficient ongoing success. *Reason* and the *facts* of a civilized society would never persecute others in the manner by which theocracies have, with such abject cruelty for those who stand on the *integrity of personal rationale.* Is it not of the highest order of shame that many religions and theocracies, these so-called standard-bearers of good, have been too often in fact the enemies of good? They are the clear enemies of liberty and freedom throughout recorded history. Therefore, it would seem fundamental and critical to maintain a separated church and state in order that liberty and freedom should thrive.

It is critical to note that some theocratic or religious individuals have yielded to no one on the side of good, due to following their own truths of good will, sacrificing their lives for good causes. Such people are the true spiritual leaders for all of us, *but in a theocracy, I may not be able to have my own opinion.* My point is this: individuals following kind and loving values learned from their religion are simply behaving well, and therefore they are great spiritual leaders, but that does not correct the core fundamental problems clearly demonstrated by theocratic faith-based rule. Separation of church and state is essential within a free society.

As nascent societies, we were born and educated on greater unknowns—less knowledge of physical cosmic laws of science and evidence—which gave easy sanction to superstitions and myth, the ramifications of which are intrinsically embedded in our human societies today. That early human phase of development stands on the pillars of *ignorance and reason's* incestuous marriage, and the painful consequential results that modern-day societies are, in many ways, imbued with.

Theocracy is implicitly based on mythology standing on the shoulders of wishful thinking and self-deception. Belief in a faith without evidence, *which may be true or not*, must be a personal journey, never imposed onto others, as that only makes it artificial. However, that is what a theocracy does; by law it imposes faith onto others.

In a decent and moral world, personal beliefs and judgments based on faith, *as opposed to reason or fact,* have no place in law or as an intrusion into someone else's personal choices.

Historically and generally speaking, a theocracy is an incomplete quest for truth, controlled by a few and thrust on the many through many forms of coercions, subtle and overt, by those in power. Fundamental theocracies will always deny the *science of reason* its factual reality unless besieged by data that are incontrovertible by even a two-year-old, and even then sometimes they will not yield to evidence. This behavior of religious fundamentalists defines the very term *irrational,* for which we often commit non-faith-based people to criminal or mental institutions, yet we give those of faith a pass and even legitimacy within our political and educational institutions. Is this nuts? Of course it is, relative to objective rational thinking.

We, as a species, clearly do not have fully developed mental facilities. Perhaps we have been so mollycoddled with anecdotal Pollyanna panaceas for answers to life's fundamental unknowns that we have culturally disconnected our responsibility to integrity.

Reason, per se, is perhaps always an infant and incomplete, but stands on the shoulders of humility and a reaching to the truth through evidence. This quest for truth through *reason* will never allow the denial of personal faith of an individual, unless that faith is physically harmful to someone else. The science of reason is true spirituality, both through the quest of the inner mind to search the power of a possible supernatural realm and the science of nature itself to understand our origins. The physical world we exist in—the very physics of that world as seen by many of those of reasoned minds—is the face of and the quest for a god itself.

- *Notes regarding the word* God*:*

  I use the term God *in a generic manner, or perhaps, better said, in a poetic manner, to identify something more than what we know, an infinite concept, unknowable to our finite existence. I do not use* God *personally to refer to a deity, as many, but not all, theocrats would generally define it. However, perhaps a deity or creator is best described as the unknown or infinity itself.*

  I also use God, *in this book, primarily as a frame of reference for seeking what is good. I do not use the word* God *to in any way signify God's existence or to deny God's existence.* God *is a good term to represent the principle of good, such as in the phrase "a godly behavior."* This is a critical point in understanding my view of God and religion.

Many theocrats today still jeopardize the world of reason, just as they did when the biblical assumptions of the earth were thought to be the center of the universe, in which the earth was only six thousand years old, the sun revolved around the earth, and the world was flat. To ignore these theocratic edicts would have summarily brought the swift wrath of torture and death from many theocrats for using the science of reason, rather than theocratic belief systems, as spiritual truth.

Theocrats of some religions, such as Buddhism, which does not believe in a deity, and others do have a more benign approach to power, which is antithetical to the monolithic religions on the planet today, such as Christianity, Judaism, and Islam. These predominate monolithic religions are predicated on doctrines written by a so-called deity, a god himself, through the hands and words of so-called inspired infallible humans. In reading this dogma, one can find almost any position to support, whether it is advancement of slavery or the killing of infidels, heathens, or heretics; see Leviticus in the Judeo-Christian Bible, or several places within the Quran. Also, contrary positions are replete in these religious dogmas toward more loving behaviors, such as the turning of your cheek under any form of evil done to you and loving others under any circumstance.

Some of this dogma is flat-out ludicrous and patently evil, and some of the dogma is supremely humane. Yet it is all called holy or divine. Troubling is the point that these human-made documents are highly respected by true believers of these religions. People of a reasonable and pragmatic approach to life should be troubled by the absolute intransigence of thinking afforded by theocracies. For instance, these positions of killing all who do not believe as I do are simply not negotiable. These are doctrines written in both the Judeo-Christian Bible and in the Islamic Quran. They disallow communication, replacing it with submission or death, if read at an absolute and fundamental level, by my understanding.

A critical evaluation of these historic documents would certainly require modification and rejection of much of the rhetoric regarding slavery, killing of non-believers, and personal lifestyle choices not relevant to kind, loving, and decent behavior. However, many fundamentalists will never give ground to words written by so-called *believers* from centuries past, and consequently we have what I consider as identity troubled-people believing in torturing, submission, and control, or some part thereof, as godly or good behavior.

Some followers of these religions have reasoned-out positions that are selective, drawn from the fundamental heritages of their religious elders and previous or current cultures. For example, some focus on the loving aspects of their doctrines and lead decent lives. Still others find glory in the more cruel and self-righteous aspects of their doctrines, and justify them as godly and righteous, regardless of the horror and selfish will they impose on others. Even the New Testament condones slavery in the books of 1 Timothy 6:1, Colossians 3:22, and Ephesians 6:5 by the instructing of slaves to be good to their masters. This is abjectly wrong at its core, yet culturally immature moments in history make pawns of the many (masses or us) and cause integrity to go into hiding, saving its head from being cut off, literally, by fundamental theocrats.

Yet just think about those who would argue today that these human-made religious documents are somehow manifestly divine and, therefore, should be unequivocally adhered to. If true, the earth would need to be viewed as the center of the universe, slavery would be acceptable, and to kill non-believers would be blessed. After all, remember the Bible says that God or truth is "the same yesterday, today and tomorrow." Taken literally, such cruel abominations and implausible ideas would be acceptable practice and facts today. Catholic priests who were allowed to marry for hundreds of years would still be afforded marriage, and so on. For the sanctity of hypocrisy rampant in mankind and theocratic institutions, these words of believing in what was true yesterday, today, and tomorrow, within theological circles, are but mere words, used to dupe and mislead us, the masses of the world.

I am not sure they were always meant to mislead on an intentional level, but ignorance leads to the same harsh and errant results. Clearly these religious documents, be they the Quran or the Judeo-Christian Bible, are only wonderful relics, often not fully intact or capable of representing a completely accurate history, as they illustrated some of the times and cultures the ancients built their beliefs and rules upon. It is important to recognize that these documents, however accurate or otherwise, are the prime source of much of the moral and structural foundations underpinning our civilization. Clearly, some of this historical foundation contains great value for the good of civilization, and some of it is a poison of the cruelest measure.

To believe that such historic documents are sacrosanct and somehow God's inerrant words is beyond all critical rationale. I argue this point given the history by which these documents were derived through human beings, errant transcriptions, theological bias, and competing religious interests, to name only a few of the variables that produced these works.

By the way, I do very much believe that truth or a God would be the same *yesterday, today, and tomorrow*, but I believe this from a point of principle—from my faith in goodness, *which does not change*. I, however, would not believe in such a position of faith as outlined in religious canons that resulted in witches being burned at the stake and heathens or infidels killed or tortured, along with other behaviors and beliefs that are implicitly cruel, and additionally would mean slavery and the inequality of human beings would be acceptable today. Such a description of good or God is incongruent, a heinous fallacy of faith in the first degree. All one has to do is read the Bible or any other works written that speak to inequality and impart harm to those who believe other than what someone else's faith dictates. Such works speak for themselves. The inhumanity manifest in portions of these documents from ancient cultures and religious beliefs should give anyone of conscience great pause.

Faith that has any real value comes from conscience, not dogma, comes from morality not convention, comes from the soul of integrity. Any other faith is blind and unholy, as it lacks the roots of goodness, of reason, and of decency, from which pure hearts can only exist.

The birth of *reason* with scientists, such as Copernicus, Galileo, and others, was a clear logic-based alternative to the sheer inhumanity that theocracies imposed through religious wars, the heinous torture of the Inquisition, the great cruelty of the witch hunts, and the Christian Crusaders' evil brutality. These forms of human slaughter in the name of God eventually found disfavor with the masses and political leadership and gave way to greater reason as a means to rule one's life and societies. Truly the work of God in the hands of theocrats was a heinous slaughter of humanity and denial of truth, which the rise of science and reason helped counter to bring greater peace and mercy into the world.

America was founded, in part, to rid mankind of religious persecution, and the US Constitution was established with that in mind. Much of Europe is today even more insistent on the division of church and state in order to never see that holocaust on humanity unleashed again. Such mass exterminations in the name of Allah or God should speak deeply and profoundly against the rule of theocracies.

However, today, we see a resurgence of theocratic fundamentalism, especially in the Islamic world but also in the Christian fundamentalists as well. These fundamentalists promote intractable behaviors of thought that rule out communication or understanding as a means for living together, but rather impose the harsh coercion of thought and behavior, or suffer exile, verbal admonitions, torture, and death.

In this modern day, such faith-based belief systems are a sign that we are not so advanced or modern, but are still struggling with warring powder kegs, this time made of weapons of mass destruction (WMD) and increasingly accessible into the cruel hands of the ignorant, selfish, and cultural theocratic lunatics.

Fundamental theocracy based on the ancient literal doctrines of books written by humans in less knowledgeable times, which are interpreted as the literal word of a God, is simply on its objective face both silly and terribly dangerous. The world of nations should require that education be improved to instill reason and true critical thought, or the theocratic selfish madmen of the world will soon have the means to take us all out.

And given the opportunity, they will.

One person's spiritual blaspheme is another person's spiritual truth, and all of this is based on faith. Tragically in parts of the world today, people kill people for these mere differences of belief in faith.

Many fundamentalists believe killing is a fundamental right to stop the free speech of others.

This behavior is a crime against humanity. If allowed to stand without the world's absolute and unequivocal condemnation, we are allowing the inmates, the religious fanatics, to hold the world hostage, and condemning freedom, truth, and liberty to certain death.

The solution to arrest this issue of cruelty about to possibly besiege the world through new WMD technologies in the hands of ignorance and cruelty is for world leaders of nations and religions to speak with clarity and solidarity. If a religious leader or government is known to issue an edict of physical harm or death on an individual or state for the exercise of freedom of speech, then such an individual or government should be condemned by the world community of nations and altered or abolished, and the participants held to account before an international tribunal for crimes against humanity.

Theocrats and ideologues who would commit harm via suicide attacks or other torturous means are not any different than you or I on the surface. Some are intelligent, some are disciplined, some are simpletons, and some are a combination or part of all of these attributes. What makes them different is their lack of integrity (individuality) and the fact that they are mere pawns, committed to a cause that has lost all individual rationale. Their rationale is flawed without reason, as it is founded solely in faith. Faith when unchecked allows human beings to hate, to become selfish, to ignore common decency, and all of this evil is often predicated on words written in so-called holy writings that give these pawns the ability to justify actions without factual evidence.

This has been in large part the unfortunate essence of theocracies and many of the underpinnings of religions themselves, which have, through the ages, created books written by humans, but which are given divine sanction, without ongoing review and honesty. This is a fatal flaw of power itself. As has been said, *absolute power corrupts*, and theocratic organizations exemplify that point. Theocrats and their base of support are without integrity, as they are the pawns of culture, of humankind, and of their own self-indulgence, all justified by way of ignorance and fallacious answers to life's unknowns, established by their perhaps well-intended elders, superstitions, and mythological beliefs.

So a question arises: How does a social environment, such as a democracy, in the broad sense of the term, which believes in communication, open thought, and the basic premise of "*do no harm*" to other sentient beings, couple itself with a structure not built on evidence and evaluation, but on faith, which allows for the torture and killing of others who communicate other than the way in which you do?

This is the current modern-day dilemma with the so-called terrorists and religious fanatics of all stripes. We have failed to arrest the religious failures of the past through the lessons of heinous behavior from the religious inquisitions and the previous religious wars, to the point where we have let these religious extremists rear their heads once again. Societies have failed through respect for the various faiths and many of their intrinsically good values, forgetting that faith also has rhetoric and history premised on control, slavery, and killing as well. This is true in the three main religions of today—Islam, Judaism, and Christianity—in a time when weapons are no longer deployed simply one on one. Now billions of humans can suffer by the acts of one faith-based servant of God or Allah by way of WMDs.

It is true that ignorance of the masses was once a tool of leadership, both religious and secular, to control and manage the masses, but today, allowing ignorance within the ranks of the masses can destroy us all.

Society must find a clear presence of mind to glean the good from the great faiths of the planet and eradicate the blind faith to these ancient mythological religions, or we will suffer the very *curse of evil* by our own cowardly, ignorant, and thoughtless actions. The leadership of the world must find a way to educate the masses to think critically. Otherwise, religion and all of its good intentions may damn us, through its many cruel and evil legacies, to ignorance, misery, and death.

This is very much the world we live in.

I have to conclude that human intellect has not progressed much and is neglecting the lessons of history about such theocratic governments existing today or the former cruel Christian crusaders and Islamic wars. Centuries of popes have sanctioned torture unto death of non-believers. In past and current periods of history, religion has darkened the truth and reason of all mankind through notions of a possible god's truly cruel and wrathful nature. In time, mankind's intellect and courage rose to free us, and it appears that a resurgence of thoughtful intellects need to take that courageous step again to right one of mankind's greatest hypocrisies against humanity and right the world ship of state.

The alternative is very bleak, given the capability of modern-day weapons in the hands of one ideologue or theocratic fundamentalist to massacre the many—at the behest of a God who allowed instruction for these torturous acts in ancient and suspect texts written and transcribed by mankind and used as inviolable documents throughout the centuries.

I would point out that moral relativism, which is lacking in doing no objective harm to others, if considered acceptable to some individual or culture, is the equivalent to religious fundamentalists who would without forethought execute so-called religious laws without judgment as to the impacts of actions.

Today, these so-called divinely written texts certainly reflect some thoughtful and profound mores, but also have cruel bents born of cultural proclivities, the competition for power, and worst of all, the dogma of a wrath-filled *god* that lacks all moral ethos. It is the paragon of absurd to describe a god who lacks moral virtue, yet that is the god described by many ancient scriptures. One could argue that demagoguery was at its pinnacle in, if not born of, these times, when cloisters of biased monks or singular authors manifested these texts on how to live life. More interesting is that we, with the lessons of history to draw from, do not more critically examine the merits of these texts in lieu of the blind-faith acceptance demonstrated by the masses. This blind obedience is misguided by some decently intended people, who, through an attempt to be obedient to a cause, rally to that cause to the point of losing all rationale. Consequently they lose their integrity. Some of these *believers* are not as decent as others and have some real failures of conscience, which by way of ignorance or malice border on gross negligence and a complete failure of personal moral decency.

The question arises: How do intelligent people so docilely accept these religious texts and theocratic leaders as infallible and absolute? Especially when the evidence by scholars is overwhelming that these religious texts are written not by inspired words of Providence, but by the interests and personal beliefs of human beings? Much of these archaic texts are replete with cruelty, slavery, and standards of inequality that have no place in a godly, decent, or moral world.

Enlightened? *We as a collective people clearly are not.*

Thinking about this subject and humankind's intellect reminds me of another fellow, an independent thinker whose wry humor abounds on the subject of religion and the human race. His humor, I believe, is unrivaled and poignantly important. Here is one of his indelible quotes:

Such is the human race, often it seems a pity that Noah . . . didn't miss the boat.
—Mark Twain

Chapter 5

CHRISTIANITY AND OTHER RELIGIONS

It is incomprehensible that God should exist, and it is incomprehensible that he should not exist.
—Pascal

It is important to note that this chapter often refers to what I consider an assumption of who and what Jesus was about, coupled with Christianity and other religions. For instance, the ancient manuscripts of record that document Jesus vary in the details about who and what he was and what he believed in. Early Christianity had several branches, some believing in multiple gods, differences regarding what constituted salvation, women's roles in the church, Jesus's very divinity, and much more. Had a different branch of Christianity prevailed, the teachings from our churches today would clearly have been different. Therefore my assumptions of Jesus in this chapter may, in fact, be naïve and wrong, as there is no way to know the actual truth about times past—especially given the varied thoughts contained in the thousands of documents from and about those ancient times.

I use this Golden Rule benchmark to align with what I believe are similar assumptions from these religions and their ascribed leaders, such as Muhammad, Moses, and Jesus. So, as I describe what I believe some of these religious leaders assumably said, I am solely focused on my analysis as to how their behavior or words measure up to goodness or godliness, if you will. I acknowledge this is a one-sided filter of the complete facts and with a clear bias. Keep in mind that I cannot know the actual facts.

Foremost I am interested in what I define as good values from these ancient religions and their leaders' and advocates' recorded thoughts. My definition of *good* is what I believe is a general archetypal human edict—the Golden Rule and humane justice. Simply stated again, *good* must be loving and charitable, and premised not on vengeance, fear, or eternal damnation to non-followers or non-believers, but based upon decent, altruistic, and forgiving modes of behavior and acceptance. This is how I analyze and measure the teaching of these religions for the good they have to offer.

Therefore, an essential point of this chapter is not to validate or invalidate the merits of religion, their leaders, or God—even when it seems as if that is what I am doing—but rather to glean from these religious texts the loving universal values that may have been the true intent from these religions leaders and their belief systems. Much of the attributed statements in these ancient texts reads with such profoundly loving maxims and intelligent perspectives they ring true to me. It is this paragon of thought, this perfect symphony of reason, which I take from these religious texts and expound upon with my own perspectives as they relate to goodness. I also acknowledge fully these texts are coupled with what I would describe as pettiness, cold and insensitive disputes between so-called believers and other so-called believers, each calling the other false prophets, doing battles in very pejorative manners (hell and damnation to you heretics), inversely acting in ways far removed from sound pastoral and loving ways toward their philosophical opponents. Additionally I find no value in ritual or beliefs, in what is simply not knowable for me, as I would categorize this as belief in superstition and mythology; whether true or not, it digresses from the point of good behavior and doing good for good's sake. The relevance of rituals, such as blood sacrifices, is beyond what I can actually reason and thereby know to have a value beyond superstition.

To establish what is relevant, I must determine what constitutes good behavior before acting on it; otherwise, integrity is forfeited. And without integrity, I could not trust myself. In other words, if I were to blindly follow traditional rituals and beliefs, which are based on faith, not reason or knowable facts, then that behavior would lack relevance to me, as there is no direct value related to goodness or good behavior. If I acted out of such forms of blind faith, then I would be acting without integrity, and as such, it follows that I could not believe in myself or in others who behaved that way.

Historical study shows us that many current religious books, such as the New Testament, are primarily the result of oral discourse over decades, written down at later dates with known errors and suspected forgeries ending up in our canonized scriptures, at least within the Judeo-Christian Bible. If the texts written in these holy books illustrate good behavior, as I have chosen to identify it by way of the Golden Rule and altruism, then they may have merit. If they are of another color in the spectrum of values, one of vengeance, the imparting of misery, destruction, and pain, then I must call them unjust. Reason and common decency make this so.

I focus on and define behaviors and words I find good. Whether it was the original intent of the principle teachers or scribes is not important; only the intent of what is being shared and taught is of importance. That is the prime point of this chapter. As you will read, I take what a teacher such as Jesus may have said, and if it holds value for humanity, I accept it.

My understanding of religion and theocracies, primarily those of the three great monolithic religions, Judaism, Christianity, and Islam in their fundamental forms, are not intended to give cause to anyone to believe that I find these religions without moral merit. No one should believe that by citing historical facts or reasonable facts of religious history or my personal points of view of religions' fundamentalist bents, I do not find these moral efforts of the past not to be of value.

To the contrary, I would give great deference to many more substantial intents of goodness from these religions and their disciplined sense of values, understanding, and forgiveness for both the innocence of life and the guilty in life. In my view, these religions embody some forms of an archetypal humanity, which in their best moments speak to the highest of values one could aspire to. Many of the people involved with religions today are the finest people anyone may ever know. However, I also acknowledge, as I have before, that many of these religions' so-called divine scriptures are wrought with ill will, personal dogma, and writings of a god who uses natural disasters, built into the natural evolution of the universe in the form of volcanoes, tectonic plate movements, and asteroids, to bring horror, destruction, cruelty, suffering, and death to humankind.

It is this latter set of writings from these religious scriptures that attempt to create, at best, a parable, for reasons one must decide for oneself. Or, at worst, they were written as political and personal dogma and are the personification of evil, as they speak of enslavement and control without mercy, or rewards for the faithful with ludicrous treasures of flesh or riches by participating in acts I find to be unconscionably cruel.

Additionally, God is often foremost used to deny personal freedom of choice: *For if you do not believe as I do (the church of choice), you will be damned for eternity.* Who would choose eternal damnation—if it were true? No sane person would.

Suppose first—for a moment—that a God would expect individuals to accept the notion and cruelty of eternal damnation. Second, an individual would be required to support a presumption that requires a belief in faith without reason. Logically that would require an individual to sacrifice his or her integrity in support of faith over reason. Doing so, however, would make an individual artificial and insincere in both beliefs and actions, as he or she would have to accept that lying to oneself were a *good* behavior. Hence, a human being would really not have any free choice. The whole argument in support of faith over reason is spurious. Faith is a quality of belief that comes from a true heart, spirit, and personal commitment born of reason, that doing good in life is better than doing harm. It is simple ethics. The god in these religions, as portrayed by the majority of clergy past and present, is not a reasoned representation of God or of what faith really requires of an ethical person. If so, then this representation I have just laid out defines God as not much more than a petty, cruel, jealous, selfish entity.

God or the notion of a god in its best form, is a faith in something more than what we are and a commitment to work for that goal of perfection, whether real or not, by way of living a thoughtful, caring life. To read and study the writings of the ancients is to understand mythology, superstition, and the cultures they spawned. Those ancient texts are certainly not representative of any omnipotent god by any semi-objective review.

Anyone who would believe that a god of good/love is a god who would join sides in a war or join in the horror and barbarism that humans are capable of through fundamentally adhering to the full religious texts of Judaism, Christianity, or Islam is an unfortunate individual—and worse, a potentially harmful individual.

Think about it: Damned for eternity because god made an imperfect human being? Therefore, this omnipotent god is going to eventually sweep his damaged goods under the rug and torture them forever? That is a fairytale of frightening proportions when you realize how many people actually believe this—and they may be otherwise good and intelligent people. Most troubling are the fanatics who believe this. After all, if you are a fundamentalist, then all bets are off on behavior, since vengeance, killing, and slavery are saintly to fundamentalist religion when the texts are read without exception. Women, even in the more kindly western traditions of Christianity, if the church operated at a fundamental level should cover their heads and never speak within a church (see Corinthians and Timothy in the New Testament). However, if you read about the early history of the Christian faith, women were instrumental in its propagation, leadership, and support, even approved of by Paul and Mary Magdalene, who Jesus held as his favorite according to a few disciples like Peter and Philip. However, as the church began to take root, women were literally erased and removed from positions of importance. Read *Lost Christianities* by Bart Ehrman for a scholarly review of the various branches of early Christianity.

Many of these ancient writings, or later chronicled events, that allow for cruel behavior in our religious texts written ages ago, from my point of view, are literally written by actual *infidels and heathens*, by selfish, misguided, or delusional human beings using the fallacious fear of God to control others. For the most part, these ancient texts are not of any god I would abide by, as I could not in good conscience sincerely be a party to the cruelty and inequality ascribed in these texts.

My god, if I could actually know one exists, would be of a higher nature. It is the idea of that higher nature that I follow today, and it is called by a few names, such as *decency*, *conscience,* and *reason*. It is my faith in these human attributes of actual free choice and thoughtful actions that drive honest behavior. If I acted good only to avoid punishment, I would not have free choice; I would simply be a lab rat responding to stimuli. Needless to say, human beings are more than that. If you believe in a god, I would suggest god is more than that as well.

I actually do not believe one can know if there is a god, from my point of view, since I am a finite being and a god would be infinite. As a matter of physical fact, a finite being cannot know all things, since finite means you have limitations; thereby you are defined into a particular space and time. Conversely, infinite structures cannot be defined, as they have no boundaries. In fact, they are not structures, as they are simply *all*, which is not knowable to a finite being. For to know what *all* or *everything* or *infinity* or *God* possibly is would be to define it, therefore putting perimeters around it and limiting it to a finite existence. *Even the Judeo-Christian Bible is replete with references telling the reader that you cannot know God, that God cannot be fully understood.* Fundamentally it is not possible for a finite being to understand or know if a god actually exists, since that would give limits or definition to God and therefore God would no longer be infinite. As a direct result of these facts, we have the import of faith regarding religious belief. Since God cannot be evidenced by knowledge, then faith (belief without evidence) is the only way a human being can have a belief in a god.

"A comprehended God is no God."—Dio Chrysosotom (40-120, quoted in Mencken, *Treaties on the Gods*, chapter 5)

I would argue that a God, in practical terms, is simply a reference to faith in love/goodness, positive forms of behavior versus negative or cruel behavior. I believe this is what Jesus, one of the greatest known teachers of love and goodness, believed in. In many references, he referred to himself as the son of man, not as the son of God. He is even recorded as asking, "Why do you call me good? When there is none good but that of the Father [God]." From my point of view, Jesus was saying that goodness stands on its own; it is not of individuals, but God is the transaction of good itself, *the helping of someone infirm to cross the street, and so on.* The transactions of goodness are God manifested. The transaction of good is not for self-adornment or for self-righteous personal claims, which Jesus denounced, from my point of view, by asking people not to think of him as good, but only of what he did as good. Additionally, Jesus's divine status came hundreds of years after his death, which was based on the will of a vote of mankind, not an act of any God. The documents within the Judeo-Christian Bible and many other religious documents are based on input from people, not from tablets or scriptures written by a god. At least we do not have any such divinely inspired documents, as the original manuscripts of the gospels and letters of the Bible have largely not been located or authenticated. In other words, much of the ancient documentation is presumed second-, third, or fourth-hand transcription. Additionally, critical to this issue is that the early Christian churches' beliefs were handed down through oral means for several decades before the gospels were actually documented in writing.

My personal faith is simply found in making the decision to choose doing right. My faith in love and goodness or positive forms of behavior versus vengeful or negative cruel behaviors is in the tradition found in Jesus and all great teachers and participants devoted to goodness. *Note:* When I refer to Jesus-like behavior, I define that not in the tradition of the religion that was established in his behalf, which I find often removed from truth or goodness, but within the tenets of goodness.

This act of faith I have taken can only be a personal journey, never imposed on an individual by others, yet religions throughout the ages have coerced their followers through torture and fear. Clearly the ancient rock upon which much of Christianity is built is a foundation of torture and fear. This is the antithesis of any image of a god that in good conscience I could believe in. Coercion would actually preclude authentic faith. And yet fundamentalists of all the great monolithic religions have often fed and bred their very existence by the modalities of fear and cruelty, with a pinch of non-altruistic love, through their do-as-I-say admonitions, and only then will you go to heaven.

Again, I can only see this as antithetical to the nature of any loving god I could in theory ever serve. I suppose by default, through my choices in life, I attempt to serve a god, *should there be one*, who will be a loving god, who does not allow suffering, cruelty, and injustice. It is in this form of *humanistic faith*, which someone might say I believe in, a poetic reference to God through values engaged by integrity. *One of the greatest historical models of this integrity would be the description of Jesus, as I have described him, not as he actually might have been.*

The alternative to integrity in your faith toward behavior selection is to create an artificial person who is motivated by the fear of hell or damnation, not by virtue itself. If I say I believe in a god, it is not that I can know that there is a god, as I stated earlier, but that hypothetically a god would foremost be a god of love who values *integrity* (Latin for *individuality*), and in that integrity I would be personally bound to seek goodness.

The claims that goodness or god would ever be manifest by the killing of heretics, heathens, infidels, or firstborns, or the killing of communities through god-induced floods, plagues, or other natural disasters, could be justified because an omnipotent god wanted to have company around by creating people with free will, is imaginative rhetoric that seems to have been pulled right out of the air. The consequences of such rhetoric regarding free will, which people have enunciated in a possible god's behalf, was that because of free will, God had to allow the Adolph Hitler's throughout history to practice genocide and torture millions, and that God weeps at such events, is a grotesque use of cognitive license. *I have probably not heard it all, but pretty darn close.* There are many inventive rationales to try to make sense of horror and of a god's supposed part in it. Some of these events are written in historical religious texts, and some of them are pure pulpit conjecture, but all of these rationales and behaviors allowed in the name of Allah or God or intended by God are not of goodness, but of evil.

Right and wrong are not hard to understand in this regard. Evidence of cruelty coupled with my faith in support of good actions is what binds me to this inescapable conviction of right and wrong. It is just that plain and simple.

Truthfully, no one can ever actually know who God is or if God exists; hence, in addition to faith, is the advent of the agnostic, whose personal integrity confines him or her to this inescapable logic. Secondly, since God is a singular (infinite) entity, and since infinity, or omnipotence, encompasses what is indefinable, a human being can only exist within a dual realm. In other words, a human being is a mere *province of the whole.* Another way to express it would be to say a human being is *one* (finite) element inside of another *second* element (infinity), thus the dual nature of humankind. A human is both the *knower* (finite) and part of the *knowledge* (infinite)—in contrast to a God, who would only be the knowledge (singular), encompassing all things.

Duality and singularity are opposites, just as light and dark are; they cannot be reconciled. To be singular, to attain one's god or infinite state, you must give up self, ego, knowledge of self, and existence as a human being, thereby transcending to the infinite. Extinction becomes ultimately infinite. This is an absolute paradox and conundrum for anyone to comprehend. But then that is what infinity, or God, is—completely unexplainable, all time, all space, without limits past or future.

I was raised with the Judeo-Christian King James Bible as my prime cultural standard. As a result, I am most familiar with it. I am much less familiar with the Quran; however, I have read a portion of its passages and absorbed knowledge from a reading of history and the current Islamic fundamentalist behavior and comments in our world today. One of the great quotes of the Islamic faith comes from the greatest of known Muslims, Muhammad (570–632): *"All God's creatures are his family; and he is the most beloved of God who does most good to God's creatures."* The core tenets of that statement are as genuine as one can be toward the highest of ethical and loving values. Nowhere in that statement is there the means to do harm to others. If we could throw out all of the other rhetoric associated with all religions and focus on this core statement, we would embrace goodness, or God, in the highest of forms for those who believe. This is the equivalent to the Judeo-Christian Golden Rule and having a pure and sincere heart.

However, since my background is clearly more knowledgeable with the core tenets of Jesus, as I understand him, perhaps not as he actually was, rather than Muhammad, he still is my model for living life, notwithstanding his clear belief in a God and many Jewish religious traditions. I have not embraced the religious context that has been established on his behalf; I have only embraced the core importance of his basic humane teachings. Jesus, according to what we know of him, lived in a *way* that brought one to greater *truth* and a more decent *life.* That may be an oversimplified or false perspective since there is much scholarly review that Jesus was perhaps a victim of his cultural times and less a true individual, with all sound values at his core. However, regardless of any imperfections one might claim in him, I see his ideal example for life as inspiring and good. His core values, which as I have stated entail *the Golden Rule and forgiveness*—and anyone else who follows those same values—will manifest the following: to love your enemies, to forgive, and to treat others as you would like to be treated yourself. Jesus appeared to engage in a greater integrity and brought light to a dark and less-understanding period of time in history, where for the most part, both secular and religious doctrinaires ruled primarily by fear.

I believe I can safely assume that if such a person as a Jesus were here today, he would create as much havoc to the current church's dogma as he did to religion two thousand years ago.

In preaching the Golden Rule, Jesus implicitly preached that *unless you have love in your giving*, in your actions of intended good, your goodness and your actions are insincere and worth nothing. In other words, his message said that if your actions are to gain favor or grace, you will always lose. If your actions are to do good for good itself, you will gain everything. (Refer to Corinthians 1 chapter 13, verses 1–3 for a biblical example of what I am attempting to describe; see appendix A.)

Yet the Christian religion that was founded in his name has been morphed, extrapolated, manipulated, and perverted in Bible texts and pulpit opinions to the theme that unless you bow to me (generally some denomination of a church) in words, by accepting Jesus as Lord, and in some cases, do all forms of human-made rituals, you will go to hell. That motivational premise violates God and the principles of Jesus. The fundamental lessons of Jesus are that if your heart is pure, so are you. All of the other philosophy and human-made dogma, either from Jesus or from those representing his message, that reaches beyond this simple ethical premise *of a sincere motive,* is certainly not of essential value.

Again, I review documentation through the filter of values I believe to be universally good. This view I harbor sees this teacher Jesus in a manner that is universally good, not selectively good. This may very well be my Pollyanna reading, but even if it is, these ethical notions I hold to are certainly present in the underpinnings of Christianity's message.

Unfortunately, the modern church interprets such acts of simple ethically based goodness as essentially empty, by saying that *works* alone will not make you *saved*, but faith and works together will. Well, I agree with that, but I use what I believe to be Jesus's interpretation or actual manifested works and faith, not the mainstream church's outline of Christian-like behavior regarding works and faith.

For example, faith in good for good itself is *real faith.* This form of faith demonstrates by action a nature of a God or godliness; then, and only then, will your works be sincere and have true value. However, the church today tries to imply that faith means having faith in giving up your integrity to believe, without evidence, in their dogma, by committing yourself to the arbitrary act of accepting Jesus as Lord, and then and only then will your works be of value.

The actual acceptance of Jesus is manifest by virtue of accepting his way of approaching and living a loving life, not in siding with the church that he is God, a notion not settled as canon law until centuries after his death. One method of faith asks you to believe that doing good for good itself seeks the kingdom of God, in whatever way an individual might define the term God. The other method of faith suggested by the church simply ratifies the dogma of the church and misleads itself away from the faith Jesus asked people to devote themselves to, *the faith to give for goodness's sake, regardless of reward or merit*—and to do it with a pure and giving heart, as any offering of faith otherwise, such as given for reward, would be empty and false (see appendix A). This is the *common denominator* that I believe Jesus espoused in embracing everyone who believed in good for good's sake, and then followed through by actions or works. Had the Christian world taken a different course and followed this kind, loving behavior, it would have spared the world many of the atrocities humanity has suffered in the last two thousand years in the name of the church as it coerced and tortured many of its converts.

You decide what is correct when it comes to faith: *personal integrity* or *following others?* Which is the true ingredient for the faith Jesus spoke of?

Note: The gospel of Thomas shares this view: *"When you come to know yourselves, then you will become known, and you will realize that it is you who are the sons of the living father"* (God). This was a gnostic Christian view, that knowledge and behavior—in and of yourself—were more essential than faith was in aligning yourself with Jesus or God.

For those of other faiths, please understand that I am not trying to indicate one representative of good or one god over another by using

Christianity's representative as an example. Christianity is simply what I am most familiar with. Foremost, I am stating that this, in an ideal sense for me, is a sound model of behavior theoretically practiced by Jesus. I admire such behavior and attempt to abide by it. It would be hard to find a better way to live, but it must be lived because it is right, not due to fear of punishment or consequence. Anyone who would attempt to live this good life to avoid a hell or gain merit points does so without a pure heart, or without love, to paraphrase Christian doctrine. I am in full agreement with that doctrine. To do otherwise would only amount to artificial sentiment, void of real value. Essentially it would be works without faith. Both are required to be genuine.

With regard to other philosophical and religious extrapolations from mankind—heaven with streets of gold, angels with wings, and hell with fire and Satan with horns—these are mankind's creative notions, imaginatively extrapolated and leveraged to control with fear and reward. How one can find those Pollyanna panaceas to ease one's mind, I can only suppose. Heaven and hell are, in practical terms, metaphors, allegories for what awaits positive versus negative actions, in this world or any other unknown world. They are relative results of in-kind actions, not motivators. If a so-called god or the controller of the universe is vengeful, they are motivators; if a God is merciful, they are results. The church has greatly misrepresented the nature of these opposites, for which it clearly gains much better control of its followers. Conversely, if a church is predicated on a Jesus-like state, it would drive personal integrity and true hearts, not automatons reacting to reward and punishment stimuli.

Humankind's early cultures were obliviously awed by the nature of their own conscious awareness and the universe before them. It was natural behavior to look for a belief in something more than one's self. Leaders of early communities or tribes set the foundations for those spiritual longings. That spark of wonder in early humankind, fostered in less analytic or knowledgeable times, has been both a blessing and a curse. Nearly all forms of mythology and superstition about God were born in this manner of humankind's early longing to understand the universe. But this was from humankind's invented knowledge, not from empirical knowledge, which of course was not available to early humans; hence we have such beliefs that the earth is only six thousand years old documented in modern-day religious texts.

The genesis of sentient thought was limited in a world with minimal scientific knowledge, and within that knowledge vacuum, the tribe's leaders or spiritual leaders set the standard for their cultures. When science began to add knowledge to the former vacuum by which decisions were previously made, it often conflicted with already-established belief systems and was rebuked harshly, for the most part. It took centuries to find accommodation. Through that accommodation, our great monolithic religions have never modified their previously written texts, but have instead created new denominations that adhere to some traditional aspects and reinterpret or ignore other aspects of their religious texts. However, the fundamentalists are rooted in using all of the tools before them, handed down from cultures of a different time, regardless of the good or cruel consequences.

Actually the many so-called divine texts of these religions are a mix of paradoxes and opposites, and it is left to the readers to determine which method of behavior they will apply to themselves and to others. Will they use *an eye for an eye, and simply cut off your arm if you steal a loaf of bread, and murder you if you murder someone else? Or will they turn the other cheek and love their enemies and show mercy?* It is all there in the religious texts, for the reader to use God's will in almost any form the reader chooses.

Today in the twenty-first century, we have a new form of god entering the arena of humankind. It is called intelligent design. The premise is that the universe is so complex that it could not have evolved without supernatural intelligence behind it. Interesting to me is, how did that intelligence behind intelligent design develop? Is it not also complex? Was it not evolution from which it was created, or was it another intelligent designer? Just a question . . .

The only thing certain is infinity, which we, as finite beings, will never have the ability to understand. To understand infinity would be to define it, thereby adding limitations, which would make it no longer infinite. Infinity is the ultimate paradox, the omnipotent realm we exist in but will never understand. My primary interest here is to point out that some people are attempting to call intelligent design a science. When something is based on a belief of faith, it is not science. It is philosophy or religious or cultural studies, but not science. It should be examined and studied, but not taught as an article of evidence upon which science is based. Science is always evolving, but it is based on new data, new physics testing, new evidence, not entirely on subjective belief or faith.

The essence of religion, and what the great teachers of history attempted to bring us, was in some cases brought forward through the ages in the form of superstition and myth, much of which was tied to fear-based admonitions of supernatural gods. And conversely, some teachings brought us principles that asked for our integrity for good, not for our submission to good, to live life by that which encourages the best in us, to seek out and do the very best by everyone, and asked us to love others and ourselves, even in our failings.

I believe Jesus in an ideal sense; certainly and very simply Jesus referred to himself as a simple son of man. However, I acknowledge that even though some of the original Greek and Latin biblical manuscripts were massaged to clarify Jesus as God in our current King James and other standard Bibles, Jesus himself appears to have been a pious Jew, following the law of Moses, with his own interpretation and believing in God—and so thought of himself as doing God's will. He certainly gave of his life to do the right thing by people and serve his belief in God; and for that ultimate gift, what did mankind provide as his legacy? The less admirable side of mankind, in large part, took his legacy and used him for selfishness, perpetrating unspeakable atrocities in his name. Remember that men, not a god, decided to deify him hundreds of years after his death, in an effort, I believe, to further sanction their belief system, authority, and control over potential divergent people and social structures.

If you study how mankind promulgated these religions—fundamentally through tyranny—it is not a pretty picture. It has been a cruel, wicked, and consequently, torturous road for human beings throughout our past centuries.

And the continuing tragedy is that not very many people get it.

As cultures have progressed into our modern day, we have removed many theocratic governments, and we have found ways in almost all religions to accommodate more kindly interpretations and ignore much of the horrible reality from the religious past, save for the fundamentalists. The few theocratic governments, for the most part, in place today are not pure stewards of their theocratic laws. They have also found accommodations to meet some current civilized cultural norms, economically and spiritually. The purity of religions as they have been translated from so-called divine holy writings, if applied to life as we live today, would be unthinkable to the majority of the world. I firmly believe that stable religions, which our cultures are in large part based upon, get a pass, for the most part, from critical analysis in the world today.

One might think that the journalistic world would review the facts and consequences with more diligence. Such analysis does exist in a much larger degree in the sciences, from theology to cosmology. But that is about it. The current world, for the most part, is not addressing religion, its validity, or its consequences in any substantive manner. It is the catch-22 taboo of our times, and few will dare to examine it—far too few.

In light of humankind's checkered history in the pursuit of knowledge and understanding of itself, and the resultant fallout manifest in our varied faiths today, I consequently believe that if we would abandon all that we imagine as right and good that has been established from our heritage of thought, whether religious or otherwise, and rather adopt what we ourselves, here and now, believe is right and good without the baggage of history, we would be closer to God or the precepts of a god in the highest and most loving and healthy of forms.

In contrast, what we have today is largely ignorance disguised as truth and blindly accepted. It is unfortunate that we live in such unnecessary intellectual darkness. This darkness is ironically and predominately based on religious history, which should theoretically illuminate, not obscure, knowledge. But this is where we are.

So, by and large, humanity continues to primarily operate today and toward tomorrow on its pillars of blind historic faith, rather than from a faith in ethics fostered by critical knowledge and goodness. I am hoping, in time that will reverse itself. In so doing, the innocent and ignorant killing of so-called heretics (people who believe other than you), along with other horrific atrocities and other useless or ludicrous behaviors in the name of Allah or God, will cease.

To conclude with this subject, let me stress that many people involved with religion are well intended, and in many cases, some of the finest human beings you may come to ever know, because they abide by a moral compass of personal integrity that seeks the good aspects of their religion rather than a strict adherence to the full reading of their religious documents. Unfortunately, these good people are not the only religious faction; they are in league with those who believe in inequality and the fanatical and dangerous views also attributed to these ancient human religious texts. It is this latter group whose ignorance or cruel natures attempt to deny us freedom of thought and action, and cage us all. Decent people, or a godly people, should all be free.

As a result of the reality of the past, I hope we all open our eyes and hearts to the intended value of history's great teachers and know the difference between the self-interested noise and the clear beauty of truth. It is our integrity that will allow this awareness—and only our integrity.

The crux of our current Christianity is based on what I have described as non-essential issues, such as believing that Jesus's death was a blood sacrifice that provided a mechanism for humans to find salvation from the wrath of a God, that Jesus was resurrected from the dead, and that he was God. Firm evidence in support of such beliefs is implicitly unknown. Most important, it is unnecessary in bettering yourself for the cause of humanity or for possible alignment to a belief or a cause greater than yourself. It is worth noting that not all early Christian manuscripts supported this prerequisite of blood sacrifice for salvation, as the original Greek gospel manuscripts of Luke appear to indicate that salvation comes from simply changing one's life. Certainly this was a concept resident with the gnostic Christians, who held beliefs that were based on greater individuality and behavioral values rather than necessarily centralized authority. The disciple Luke and the Gnostics, to a large degree, had it right in my view, as an individual's free choice is the only manner in which you can be sincere in actions. To choose ethics based on admonitions, fear of hell, or arbitrary and currently unknowable faith-based beliefs is without merit. It is insincere, as it is done selfishly to gain reward beyond the joy of doing good for good itself. Doing good for good itself, rather than acting out of fear or reward, is the true strength of character, the true ideal essence of religion.

Certainly when you review the manuscripts and beliefs of the early Christians, their beliefs were quite varied: some believed that without circumcision you could not have salvation, and Peter (a practicing Jew) wanted some of his sermons and instructions withheld from the gentiles, because they would not understand and possibly misuse the information. Some early Christians believed in multiple gods, and so on and so forth. All of these various sects justified their beliefs with the teachings of Jesus. It seems apparent that many individuals and organizations simply developed their own philosophy of Jesus and God, in the best way they believed correct to receive salvation from God or the gods.

As I review this historic information, I am struck by how similar it is to much earlier mankind, as well as more modern-day primitive societies, which still engage in ritual animal killings and rituals to appease the gods to ensure good crops and good fortune. These rituals are essentially based on a *guilt-take* that God causes harm in the form of disease, famine, and natural disasters if we are not good.

This is very much the God in the Judeo-Christian Bible, and it is all clearly created by mankind's early notions of the universe. These early thought processes are what the majority of our modern civilization uses as the underpinnings for our varied cultures.

I will just sum up this chapter by proposing a logical argument, which many in the church today would agree is an argument based on reason. As I heard recently, a television preacher said, reason was essentially the roadblock to God. What else could he say when confronted with facts? And people actually listen to these theological leaders. This is very unfortunate; such self-serving rhetoric is certainly not from any god, but mankind's convenient interpretation of a god. The consequences of this leadership is to make ancient documents absolute truth, thus relegating scholars, research, knowledge, integrity, and the quest for truth to the waste bins of the unnecessary, and even, for some, to the equivalent of the damned.

For me, the logic of holding to the belief that a god would send people to eternal damnation, based on their integrity to question a set of mandates that are not knowable and are irrelevant to goodness, is not justice. It is anything but. Clearly, free choice for some people is based on uneducated decisions, and to condemn them to hell because they did not have a Harvard-level presentation of God, and so are less knowledgeable, or that their own sense of sincere integrity should somehow ordain them to eternal condemnation, is preposterous to every sensibility of right and goodness by any decent or ethical definition. This cannot be the message religion should be holding onto if it expects many thoughtful, reasoned, and loving people to continue to participate.

I can only hope that, with time, we as a human race come to understand ourselves and our religious histories with greater clarity, and that we review what spirituality means in the simplest and truest forms, thus restraining ourselves from its dilution by poisoning it with myth or superstition. I would argue such has been the case as we review history. The impacts of our ancient theologically based, agenda-driven spirituality has caused great tragedy and carnage for mankind, and it is likely to continue. The vast majority of us, whether religious or not, would obviously desire that such tragedy and carnage arrest themselves. Perhaps one way to do that is to simply understand that *spirituality,* the spirit of good, is a primary essence in all of us, albeit not always used.

There are various spirits. There are good, bad, cruel, and loving, among others. The greatest of these is that of love, of charity, born from the spirit of humility, grace, and forgiveness. It is this zestful expression of light that shines brightest in those who are truly spiritual beings, tapping into a faith in good and something more than what we might actually know. These are people who are, foremost, loving in design and commitment; whether they are part of a religious or secular foundation has no bearing. You will find these people in all walks of life: some are in the ministry or the military, some are inmates in prisons, and some are simply among the silent good Samaritans moving through our daily lives. The best of these people are manifest in times of trouble, as they embody the highest of values; they embody godliness through their grace and faith in caring for others, regardless of their own personal hardships or sufferings. All of these human beings are, first and foremost, spiritual in the truest and purest form and meaning of the word. They are not spiritual by way of dogma, but by integrity. They walk in the pure and simple definition of being *spiritual*, without addendum, agenda, or cause; they seek goodness for goodness's sake.

Religion, in its best sense, is not about the accurate accounting of history, nor its negative historic and current contributions to the inequality of classes and sexes, and to the killing, slavery, and torture of humanity. Rather, religion, in its best sense, conversely, and so ironically, has contributed to the highest of moral teachings to civilizations and individuals by way of the Golden Rule, by way of mercy, charity, integrity, faith in goodness, and love for all.

Make no mistake: many religions have the ancient rhetoric to guide us in either direction. Therefore, taking a rational stand for goodness—and by simple definition of goodness, I mean that which *does no harm*, which discriminates on behalf of freedom and responsibility, as well as doing unto others as you would have them do unto you—this is the only godly nature and science of behavior we should be gleaning from ancient religious texts and ideally committing to ourselves.

Imagine the results of doing less; we have a history of blindly doing just that.

Once again, for those interested in further review of Christianity and its development into our modern day, please read *Misquoting Jesus* by Bart Ehrman, published in 2005. Many of the Greek, Latin, Hebrew, and Coptic early manuscripts of the gospels, epistles, and letters differ from the Bible as we generally know it today in some very interesting and substantial ways. The earliest of our biblical texts, along with other gospels and early Christian beliefs, were many and varied. It took centuries of textual modifications, personal interpretations, and corrections of assumed textual errors of previous manuscripts, along with different Christian belief systems and altering text to clarify what each diverse group believed, before we ended up with the textual documents we have today. *Misquoting Jesus* is a great explanatory, non-agenda-driven scholarly review of what we know and do not know about Christian religious history. Also, Bart Ehrman has authored a number of other books just as scholarly and important.

The following verse from a song written post 9/11 sums up, very elegantly and simply, what I have taken two verbose chapters of prose to describe regarding the essence of religion and human behavior:

Until we begin to love one another, we will not reach the Promised Land.
—Don Henley, Eagles, "Hole in the World"

THINKING
RECOMMENDATION
CREATIVE
THINK
PROJECT
OPINION
BRAINSTORM
INTELLECT
PHILOSOPHY

Chapter 6

A Time for Reason

***The important thing is not to stop questioning.
Curiosity has its own reason for existing.
—Albert Einstein***

With billions of human beings believing in religious faith not backed by reason, such as virgin births, angels appearing to religious leaders, or a god who kills all firstborns but is a god of love, coupled with Noah's Ark holding every species, male and female, from all microbes and insects to all animals and all ethnic human beings, along with the sanctity of slavery, concubines, and the slaughter of thousands of witches, along with tens of thousands for heresy, primarily during the Great Inquisition, we are far from a world built upon reason. We are firmly built upon myth, legend, and superstition for billions of human beings.

As Thomas Jefferson wrote to John Adams in an 1823 letter, he believed we would find an era of reason someday. However, I believe Jefferson would be surprised how long those hopes for an era of reason would actually take.

Thomas Jefferson wrote to John Adams the following: "And the day will come when the mystical generation of Jesus, by the Supreme Being as his father in the womb of a virgin, will be classed with the fable of the generation of Minerva in the brain of Jupiter. But may we hope that the dawn of reason and freedom of thought in these United States will do away with this artificial scaffolding, and restore to us the primitive and genuine doctrines of this most venerated reformer of human errors." In other words, Jefferson believed in the goodness Jesus stood for, but was not supportive of the human-made rhetoric that was drafted by way of the organized church. Jefferson believed in fact, not fable.

The Judeo-Christian Bible or the Quran, along with other relics of ancient times used to fill the vacuum of missing knowledge, which science is helping to correct, are believed by far too many humans to hope for common sense or reason to rule the values that drive sincere decency and truth.

It is my understanding that the first five presidents of the United States were not Christians, which is understandable given the oppression and tyranny that underpinned the cultures they had broken away from by establishing America. Many of the first presidents were deists, believing in something more than themselves perhaps, and there is some belief that they were agnostic or atheist—but they were intelligent, integrity-based leaders, not bound by conventionalism or religious traditions that many in the United States seem to assume of them today.

I remember hearing that even Abraham Lincoln wrote a short book called *Infidel*, in which he described himself as an infidel because in good conscience he could not resign himself to believing that a god would persecute people for eternity. That defied his sense of decency and fairness, which resulted in him being true to himself. Just imagine if we had such a president today who described himself as an infidel.

In other words, our roots in this great country are from founders who were more than followers, lapdogs, or traditional, conventional thinkers. Rather, they were moral thinkers, a very rare and critical element that bore this great nation in brilliant words and ever improving deeds. Keep in mind our founders did not forbid religion, as they did incorporate many of the decent elements of a good religious life within our US Constitution and the Bill of Rights, but they did not support any particular religion as the foundation of this nation either.

Anyone who disagrees with this point, I would suggest that you simply review history in a raw and honest manner. I also believe the vast majority of scholarly theologians would agree with my point, that the cornerstones of our nation and the founders' belief systems that established this neutrally centered nation were not to be either a respecter or non-respecter of religion.

Religion was considered a personal journey and personal only. Religion was to be tolerated as long as it did not interfere with the laws of this nation or harm and threaten others.

However, I would argue that the societal maturity that Thomas Jefferson and his contemporaries believed would occur within time has monumentally failed. Scholars of today are aware of Jefferson's reasoning and abide by it, but the majority of the world is even more divisive and destructive by way of their religious or secular ideologies, reasoning that has blinded them to what a possible real loving god would expect from them. The "us and them" death to the infidel philosophy is obtuse to any loving or true god or decent secular principles.

Just use your reason and common sense, not your ideology, when you think, and you will easily understand that Allah or God or Reason do not condone killing in the name of god or goodness, or believe that we should ignore science, which is the true face of god and truth, as we build our human evolutionary knowledge of life.

Reason is the faith of any real possible god, just as reason is the foundation of sincere goodness. To believe in anything less is misguided, as it is based on the sands of wishful thinking, self-deception, and the insincerity of self.

Reason alone is the hope of humankind . . . but it requires honesty, not ideology. It requires personal leadership, not following others, in order to be realized. This seems contrary to the majority of humanity's history. However, all things are possible . . . *if you reason with hope!*

My hope seeks to dismantle evil, thoughtless torture, killing, maiming, and needless destruction, born of ideology, religion, culture, and differences that separate, rather than unite.

In my opinion, when we strip away all of the selfishness, rhetoric, rationalizations, and superficial materialism, we are far more alike than different. This is where reason is born—when we understand our commonalities, not our differences.

This is what is important: our common humanity, both the good and bad, not our rootless beliefs that divide us. Unity is reason. Division is the lack of all reason. Destruction is manifest by divisions, versus the warmth and goodness found in our common bonds.

It takes reason to genuinely and altruistically care. It takes ideology to divide and conditionally care.

Which road will we choose?

As Thomas Jefferson once hoped, will we choose the road of reason?

Chapter 7

ETHICS

Our very lives depend on the ethics of strangers, and most of us are always strangers to other people.
—Bill Moyers

What are the cornerstones of genuinely ethical behavior? What constitutes proper behavior? Such questions will abide in the millions.

Always the simple rule is the Golden Rule, courtesy and regard for others, even others who have so-called aberrant ways.

I know I have read or heard this somewhere, and it fits: integrity is doing the right thing, even if nobody is watching.

Culture, right or wrong, plays a huge role. Culture is actually a surrogate religion for many who do not participate in more formal religious belief systems.

Integrity (Individuality), coupled with the Golden Rule should be the principal arbiter of ethics, but unfortunately, the reality is often found in the ideological dogma of the world, its cultures, and religions, rather than from true individuals themselves. For instance, if a society believes a behavior is wrong or evil, it may instill that belief into its people and can therefore embed and make the particular behavior actually harmful, when in fact, the particular behavior, when left to itself, may be a natural and relatively harmless event.

An example is sexuality. That is the most basic of natural aspects in the nature of humanity. It is our biological birthright, the very fruit of our loins. Yet it has been the object of the cruelest of unfounded and unjustified fears and equally the most abused of behaviors.

In stark contrast, in some cultures, sexuality is celebrated and used as a way to relieve anxiety and build communities through essentially open sexual behavior. Yet in other cultures, sexuality is viewed as dark, an unspoken-of subject in public, and seen as even perverse in many instances.

Perverse, dark, hidden, not spoken of? Or open public sexuality? Is the correct behavior regarding sexuality to be found in these extreme contrasts or somewhere in the middle? What are the ethical principles for healthy sexual interaction given that sexuality is the natural physical basis for life? It is clear that many cultures have become all snarled up in knots regarding this most natural of biological and physiological acts.

Who is *ethically* correct regarding sexuality? As long as these questions surface with a reverence to review the facts, rather than with an ideological, cultural, or religious bent, these questions will find the right answers in time. It is only when such questions are approached as resolved ideological absolutes, and without understanding the context, that they will be mishandled and have a poor outcome. Ethics is not about ideology, culture, or social and religious behaviors. *Ethics is the Golden Rule.*

Watch out for the politically correct or ideological, fair-weather, traditional paradigms presented as moral absolutes. To engage without forethought in such notions of absolute morality will cause all sorts of serious mischief in the name of self-righteous correctness. Conversely, ethics makes it incumbent upon individuals to use their own gray matter when evaluating what is good and bad, before relying on traditions or current cultural solutions as inviolable.

This brief chapter concludes with five thoughts, all in complete, if not paradoxical, harmony with one another and all of which reflect on *ethics*:

For you I carried Rainbows, but forgot about my loving friends.
—Randy Dilday Sr.

Live one day at a time, emphasizing ethics rather than rules.
—Wayne Dyer

Integrity has no need of rules.
—Albert Camus

Ethics is nothing else than for reverence of life.
—Albert Schweitzer

Live and let live within the bounds of the Golden Rule.

Chapter 8

FREEDOM AND RESPONSIBILITY

While we are free to choose our actions, we are not free to choose the consequences of our actions.
—Stephen R. Covey

Freedom is a gift that can be taken away in a heartbeat if a society or a community changes. In America, the country I live in, freedom is a beacon of our heritage that has been continually evolving, and I hope America continues to always look for better ways of ensuring people's freedoms. The gift of freedom I speak of is the freedom of environment, not the freedom of the grave or the freedom of integrity. These latter two forms of freedom may both actually result in you ending up in the grave, because freedom of integrity in an unfree environment can often mean your death or at least your imprisonment and an often uncomfortable one at that.

Freedom is a gift of goodness, a birthright of a free, decent, and loving society, but it comes with a price. The price is that freedom must be applied with the same level of goodness with which it is given. It must be used with goodness in mind. Freedom granted is not the freedom to do as you will without regard for others or for sole personal gain.

Freedom becomes synonymous with responsibility. It is not a pass to simply do what you want. Freedom executed without restraint will implode on itself and create chaos, or be righted by extreme laws, putting freedom into a straightjacket. Consequently freedom's health, its wisdom, lies in responsibility of actions that promote expression but that will *do no harm* to one another.

Do no harm. What does that actually mean? How do we define it?

It means to be respectful of others, primarily by not directly imparting physical or psychological harm to others intentionally. The imparting of physical harm is often a straightforward action we can easily identify. However, psychological harm is less clear and has become the hue and cries, the motto, of the politically correct and created a whole new breed of so-called victims in society. These so-called victims have found a means to file civil suits and claim all sorts of frivolous actions should they deem another's behavior or lifestyle offensive to them.

My personal position on this is that the personal responsibility and maturity required to deal with aberrant culture or behavior is incumbent on the individual who is offended or potentially offended first and foremost. The offender should be given deference unless he or she violates very broadly held social standards or it can be demonstrated that his or her behavior is malicious. Personal responsibility is something that must be inherent in all of us. And incumbent in personal responsibility is the maturity to deal with others who may be completely innocent of actual wrongdoing other than that we dislike their behavior. Psychological harm should hold a very high threshold of proof—unless clear malice is shown—in a free society.

This is where our highest values within a human society come into play—when exercising intelligent, sensible judgment based on personal responsibility. *Personal responsibility is incumbent on both parties in any disagreement related to free choice or freedom exercised.*

This is a dilemma for many, but it is also a fundamental element of freedom. A society uses its best common sense and good judgment to solve disputes of conscience or personal offense.

Common sense and the best of judgment ultimately cannot be completely legislated; it often is best left up to the societies or individuals involved to work a dispute out, in lieu of a fixed set of laws or in a courtroom. However, if it is left up to a court, the goal should always be to follow what is right, to use common sense, not to be bound to what may appear technically right. This flexibility, this room for reason and measure, is the essence of a truly free and healthy society. It is the bedrock foundation of human beings that they are able to use judgment, rather than be solely bound by fixed law. It is important to recognize that the implicit nature of law is to protect the implied *intent* of the law, not to protect the *letter* of the law.

Freedom and responsibility, when viewed as opposites, create unholy chaos. However, when they operate as twins, they are the embodiment of decency and goodness.

- Freedom is a package deal—with it comes responsibilities and consequences.

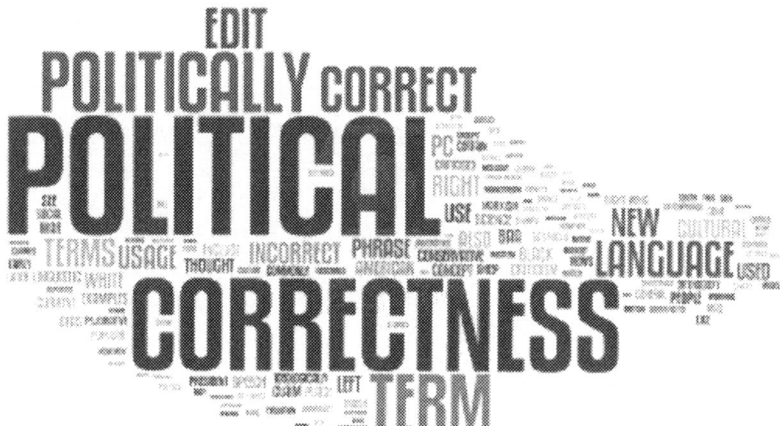
EDIT
POLITICALLY
CORRECT
POLITICAL
PC
RIGHT
USE
NEW
LANGUAGE
TERMS
USAGE
INCORRECT
PHRASE
THOUGHT
CULTURAL
CORRECTNESS
TERM
LEFT

Chapter 9

POLITICALLY CORRECT

Being Politically Correct means always having to say you're sorry.
—Charles Osgood

The politically correct! Oh, let me hold my fury! Let me find some objective approach to verbalize my view of these folks and the trouble they cause.

I may take some liberties here in this section of print to be a bit more pejorative and present my thoughts with not-always-useful language, but for hyperbole's sake and my own selfish disdain of the self-righteous in this world, I may be drawn to forgo balance and enjoy some richer language regarding these politically correct folks, who in the end, deserve respect, just as anyone does. "There but for fortune go you or I." If I were born at another end of the block or associated with different friends, perhaps I would have taken another view of life, and I hate to say it, a politically correct view! From that frame of mind, I would hope others would still love and care for me and work to broaden my perspectives and improve my behavior toward others and ultimately toward myself.

But for now I may have some pompous fun describing the self-serving and destructive ways of my politically correct friends.

Political correctness affords no quarter to honesty. It makes liars out of people. It is akin to living in the USSR during the iron-curtain era, in Iraq during Saddam Hussein's reign, or in the United States during the McCarthy days of the 1950s. You can only say what is acceptable, or you will be killed, maimed, disowned, or disparaged.

You certainly cannot be honest.

Political correctness dismantles two-way communication, much like ideologues or theocracies do: you must think as I think and behave as I do, or you will be in grave jeopardy of losing your family, your career, and perhaps, your life.

Political correctness is a demagogue's righteous indignation at its height of destructive power, based on the ridicule of others and on misinformation, manipulating the ignorant into a fevered pitch that is unfair and destructive to all that would otherwise be honest and good.

Politically correct people disable kindness. They wear their sentimental attitude heavily on their shoulders, ever looking to be kind, but they are anything but.

When I was a manager, I sometimes said in meetings that I did not want political correctness in my meetings; rather, I wanted honesty. It is critical to know how and why people think the way they do. To be a leader, to be a manager, or just to have a semblance of integrity, you cannot allow yourself the selfish luxury of being offended. It was my job to be an objective observer, rather than a victim of someone's words. Physical behavior is something else altogether, and when behavior directly imparts harm to someone else is where I draw the line between expression and actions. Thinking and expression is fundamental, essential. and incumbent to establish growth, to improve everyone. Words represent; they do not behave.

Responsibility for behavior is, first and foremost, owned by the receiver of information, not the giver. What I mean by that is, I am not responsible for how someone reacts to me, my words or behavior, if it is directed toward who I am.

If I were to hug and kiss someone in a room full of people and someone else is *indirectly* offended by that action as inappropriate behavior, that is the other person's (the observer's) responsibility to manage. I am not responsible for how other people react to me; *they are.* On the other hand, if I physically hit someone in the mouth, then I have *directly* impacted him or her with behavior and I am responsible, regardless of the actions that may have provoked the event.

Working in the corporate world for nearly thirty years, I had to periodically attend courses on ethics and sexual harassment. In one of these sexual harassment courses, the instructor used the nearly exact example above about hugging someone in a room as being inappropriate behavior because it might offend someone else. I disagreed with the instructor's argument since I do not believe I am responsible for how others respond. Other people in the course also argued that their culture instilled in them, as a courtesy, to hug and kiss people. But the instructor argued that the corporation could potentially be sued and that we were to cease and desist from any such behaviors. *Hogwash!* That was the corporate line to protect themselves. Other corporations, such as Southwest Airlines, which stands out in my mind, broke this politically correct stance and trained and trusted their employees to be smart and sensible, versus the virtual drones we were expected to be.

By the way, only a very small group of people bought into this model of conduct and people still embraced people in my former company, but the rhetoric, in many ways unintentionally, undermined the company's level of trust in its employees, which in turn diminished the employees' respect toward the business. With such rhetoric in place, this could then adversely impact the innocent, under the guise of being politically correct and proper.

If I were to be responsible for how people reacted to me, then I could not ever tell them what television shows, movies, or books I have seen or read, because they might think them politically incorrect or just wrong. These politically correct people would then be enabled to claim they were victims based on anything they disagreed with that, in some manner, offended or frightened them. This is, of course, the *cultural phase we are currently in,* which started around the 1970s, but really found its footing in the 1990s and has progressively created a whole new culture of victims.

I was born in 1950, a time when personal responsibility, rather than victimhood or the blame game, more consistently molded the culture and the character of individuals, a time when teachers were always supported by parents. Some of you will remember of what and when I speak. Believe me, these teachers did not always merit the blind trust of our parents, but it was far better than what has replaced it today, with parents blaming anyone and everyone but their children and themselves for their children's behavior. Lucrative litigation, by the way, is partly to blame, as it always is easier if you blame someone else, especially those with big pockets, like municipalities. As a result, we now have a very blame-focused society that benefits materially by playing the victim, but sacrifices integrity and self-responsibility in the process. We are raising an entire generation in this mode of consciousness that finds fault with nearly everything and believes in entitlement, which is quite the opposite of previous generations, which put greater reliance on hard work, standards, and personal responsibility.

My youthful years, in which I grew up, were a time when drama was only drama, not the overplayed melodrama that our highly competitive media and our politically correct citizens would rally us to believe today. It was our youth, using both our heads and our hearts, that brought my friends and me the wisdom to deal with the aberrant, rather than sheltered and coddled us from humanity or thought us immediate victims of another's contrary behavior. That was just life. We were expected to manage ourselves and be guided by the uncelebrated diversity in those days of measured judgments, common sense, and fundamental personal responsibility. Hence, we matured with the sense that humanity is both good and bad by nature. This paradox taught us to understand the good and bad in all people through the collective wisdom of balance, perspective, and understanding, that "there but for fortune, go you or I."

That culture has profoundly changed, or so it seems to me. As I reflect and look back, I am thankful for the values from my youth, my family, and my friends.

Speaking of teachers from my youth reminds me of a news story I saw about a decade ago, in which a seventeen-year-old girl had a sexual relationship, in fact, a love affair, with a twenty-four-year-old teacher. The mother of the girl was standing over her seated daughter at a televised news conference. The television newsperson asked if she loved the teacher, and she said yes, she did. Immediately, you could see the mother's face tighten up, tacitly implying that was not what her daughter should be saying. The daughter very timidly followed up with the thought that, "Well, what he did was wrong"—further implying that she was a victim now. The mother took over the interview after that, chastising the school and the teacher.

I tell this story, because what happened between those two lovers was not abnormal behavior when you view it generically. It was a human romance story between relatively similarly aged people. In fact, in some portions of the twentieth century and beyond, this would have been thought a delightful development in many circles. However, given our cultural times, it was frowned upon, with high shame for the teacher and automatic victim status for the student. As I remember, the student was eighteen by the time of the civil case and the news interview. And it was clear the mother portrayed her daughter as a victim, who shared no responsibility.

Had this instance happened when I was going to school, my mother and father would have, by default, put 50 percent of the blame on the student, if there should be blame, and 50 percent on the teacher. But this mother did not allow the daughter to take any responsibility. She was adamant that her daughter was the victim of a heinous act of being in a relationship with a teacher. The daughter seemed to be buying into this position, further eroding the character of this young girl. *I would put greater shame on the mother and any other parent who gives impunity to themselves and their children in similar situations.*

If these two young people did something destructive and wrong, I would have said shame on both of them. The girl at age seventeen was no child, even considering that the teacher was in a position of authority. If people will remember back a few years, it was not uncommon for people to get married at twelve and thirteen in this country, and culturally throughout history, any time after puberty was thought to be the marrying age in many cultures. Even if it is wiser to not get married so young, is it actually immoral, as one might infer from the attitudes in our culture today? I know of a woman who had just turned fourteen when she married a twenty-one-year-old man, and by age eighteen she had four children. Today, just imagine what the politically correct would have thought of this woman's husband. The standards for morality, when it comes to relationships and sex, have certainly been arbitrary. They change depending on when and where you live and who is setting the social standards. Historians will tell you that Mary, the mother of Jesus, has been thought to have married Joseph, a thirty-three-year-old man, at twelve or thirteen years of age, which was the norm in those days, and she also had several children at a young age, the first of course with the claim of a virgin birth. Yet our glorious, politically correct, who find trouble when there often is none, may have had Joseph up on pedophile or child-molestation charges if given the opportunity in today's world.

The point of these stories is not to make light of using your head when engaging in sexual behavior or when engaging in relationships that deserve additional review, but that personal responsibility and equity have all but been abandoned when we measure how to assign objective responsibility in these cases. This is in part to credence given to these new modern-day fundamentalists called the *politically correct.*

Our whole civil justice system needs better guidelines or better juries and judges, because the victim syndrome of the last couple of decades has eroded much of our common sense when deciding cases for the plaintiffs. In life, whether you decide to smoke cigarettes, drive a car, have surgery, or engage in sexual relationships, you own some share of responsibility and cannot blame everyone else for failures within your chosen engagements in life, unless malice or clear and absolute gross negligence can be proven. That is rarely the way the current system always works in reality. It should, but it does not.

When I went to school in my primary and secondary years, self-responsibility was, in my view, more fundamental, versus the victimhood that has replaced it today. In contrast, today if a teacher in some circles even touches a student, the teacher can be accused of misconduct and essentially held guilty until proven innocent. The student is almost always treated as the victim; in fact, the teachers are held up to ridicule and are impugned when they often have done nothing wrong except care enough to try to manage a given situation that required an adult's physical or verbal intervention.

When I was a young student, I believe the majority of my friends, in most cases but not all, were in general more mature in some respects, because we understood and dealt with issues that today might make a young person think he or she were somehow a victim of inadvertent and innocuous actions, and consequently fail to show any sensitivity, understanding, or responsibility in a given situation. If young people have a sound family (mother and/or father, guardian(s), etc.) that supports personal responsibility, they will be responsible, but without that strong family support, they will often take the line of least resistance. Today that line is to become a victim and leverage your youth and presumed vulnerable status in society. That is a sad reality, and the real victims are all of us in the end. Personal responsibility is important. However, *personal responsibility* is removed from the politically correct paradigm. Victimhood is understood as the norm, not the exception.

That appears to be changing. Our society is beginning to question the motives and merits of these politically correct criers. There is an emerging recognition of the apparent over-reactive hype that is often orchestrated by so-called victims today. It literally pays to be a victim; it pays to stay sick or you will lose your government benefits, and so forth. This cycle of *victim status* is becoming as indigenous to our culture as individuality and hard work once were. I hope change in our society is coming soon, because this superficial victim status most importantly debases and diminishes true heinous acts upon real victims.

The politically correct are our neo-fascists, neo-fundamentalists, and neo-ideologues disguised as utopian saints. They are insidious and lost as to how to manage themselves, let alone others. Be wary of the politically correct. As George Bernard Shaw might have put it, "They can turn truth inside-out like a glove" at the drop of a hat, and they will, if victimhood can be attained.

Honesty is a better policy.

Please do not mistake sensitivity in language for the politically correct. Sensitivity is a quality in individuals that has great value, but to stifle or sacrifice honesty for sensitivity is a critical mistake, and one that must be managed with wisdom and good sense. There are clearly vulgate, informal, and formal modalities of language. There are appropriate forums in which to engage each of them, but the politically correct have taken this concept of properly socialized behavior to excessive abstracts, which has transformed the values of self-responsibility and common sense into far less-valued commodities of behavior. Self-responsibility, self-reliance, and common sense are essential for character and appropriate action. Unfortunately our current cultural tide of an *either-or* or *black-and-white* belief system, born of the politically correct, has taken away the mix of grays that both sides of an issue have in common. It has taken away the middle ground by which personal responsibility, common sense, pragmatism, and mutual understanding operate.

The ability to reason and understand the myriad circumstances involved when making decisions is what makes us humans and not automatons. Each situation has its own set of circumstances and deserves review, sometimes mitigation and understanding, and sometimes the full weight of difficult consequences. To be human requires judgment; if it required less, we would be mere drones and robots, responding at an amoebic level to stimuli. We are not amoeba; we are evolved self-aware beings, which have a higher standard and responsibility beyond taking the simple solution and meting out laws and behavior requirements that do not also consider context.

I want to also mention how oppressive political correctness can be in group settings. For instance, in many academia circles, which can be either liberal or conservative, this stranglehold from group political correctness is the greatest of oppressions. It is based in psychological terms on *groupthink.*

Groupthink is very simply explained as when you are in a group environment where the majority thinks one way, if you do not agree with the groupthink, you are a vile pariah. Integrity is not respected in such environments, and worse, not allowed within *groupthink* organizations, save by way of pseudo-acceptance rhetoric. There is an uneasy emotionalism or outright indignation within such groups. These groups carry a very emotional edge that limits the value and execution of logical or open communication. In such groups, diversity of thought is intellectual suicide for those without a strong constitution or a wish to be possibly ostracized or demoted in their careers. You must think as the others do within the group, or you are simply a swine or worse.

You find these behaviors often in youthful groups, such as on college campuses or other almost cultish organizations that have a *holier-than-though,* rather immature, and sometimes bombastic nature. As these groups mature, they do begin to lessen their emotionalism, replacing it with understanding or respect for the other side of an issue, however appalling, as the picture of life eventually broadens for them. But as young neophytes, by way of a new job, a new subject study course, or some change in their life, which uncovers the richness of having an identity through thinking for themselves, they can awaken intellectual passions to the point of zealot-like behaviors, giving their cause an imbalance that is rebuffed for its angered/passionate indignant edge, not always for its merits. In other words, indignation and callow quests for believing in what is right often rally these individuals to causes to the point where rationality and understanding are lost. Conversely, maturity understands and demonstrates respect even for those so-called scoundrels in life, since you or I could be your very opponents simply by an unchosen different upbringing.

It is so very important to learn as soon as possible in this life that wise people clearly state the truth, but with a glint in their eye and compassion in their heart for the other person's position, for the other person is sometimes only a duped pawn opposing them. This is the bedrock of maturity and respect, which are essential components of decent enlightened sentient beings, such as Jesus, Mohammad, Buddha, Martin Luther King, the Dalai Lama, and the Gandhis and Albert Schweitzers of this world.

In other words, think before you speak, and then continue to think again and again and always admit mistakes as you continue to mature. Let your mission be humility and caring for all. In contrast, avoid being an indignant politically correct person. Political correctness more often than not only illustrates an undisciplined, unruly child, shaking his or her rattler for identity and attention, and ultimately underpins the behavior for which wars are fought. Make no mistake: we all at some point contribute to warring behavior, but we should fight the hardest of battles within ourselves not to do so.

Political correctness is a judgment-based system outside of context. It is ideologically self-righteous and one of the human race's great disgraces. The mischief these people have invoked on society through their pseudo-art of black-and-white intellectual judgment and discourse bankrupts reason while rewarding demagoguery.

It is rhetoric all wrapped up in catch-22, lily-white language that sounds good, but is anything but. It lacks understanding, balance of thought, and critical reason, extrapolating with demagoguery when any chance may arise. Political correctness also repels any honest discourse with individuals with the wrath of a psychological indignation fit for the great religious inquisitions of the Middle Ages. The politically correct do not respect opponents; they crucify them.

Political correctness is the insidious tool of either selfish scoundrels or unfortunate, poorly reasoned thinkers.

In either case, political correctness is shameful stuff.

Chapter 10

LEADERSHIP

It is amazing how much can be accomplished if no one cares who gets the credit.
—John Wooden

Leadership ideally rallies all to the cause of itself. It breeds leaders and seeks leaders who are better than itself. It knows when to give and knows when to push. Discretion and judgment, not inflexible rules, are its wisest allies.

Leadership is the gray area I have spoken of where common sense and personal commitment to self-honesty and responsibility come into play. For example, imagine a business with union and management; you find both groups have rules to abide by. If you run a business solely operating by fixed rules—management vs. union—you have solid friction, butting heads with one another, without give-and-take. This is a formula for robots, not human beings. In the best of businesses, union and management both use these rules as guidelines, not as absolutes. Give-and-take would, therefore, be the standard, not the exception. Hence, they work together in a gray area, where frictions are decreased and people are enabled to do their best. The work rules may require a break period for a worker and restrict workers to X amount of daily work hours. However, workers may be involved in a project about which they have great pride and ownership of and have chosen to forgo their break time and put in extra hours at home or at work. In turn, management sees fit to let this union employee have more freedom and flextime to manage a personal issue or grant other liberties. These are mutually agreed-to choices that benefit everyone and produce greater quality of service, products, and very importantly, personal self-esteem. This kind of relationship uses rules as guidelines to protect against abuses, but does not rule by a fixed method of operating only based on the established rules. This eliminates unnecessary friction between groups and allows the intent, not the letter, of the rule as primary.

Rules are the least effective, poorest form of an education or teaching method. Rules are primarily needed to protect against abuses. Rules are too often used by educators, management professionals, or family leaders as the easiest way to deal with an event, question, or situation. They are used too many times to allow us to skate past the important work of analyzing the merits of a situation. I will reiterate that to be human is to use judgment, not to simply react as an amoeba would to fixed stimuli, but to respond with consideration for the context in which an event occurs. This ability to measure and judge is a human attribute and a high responsibility, which we sometimes will relegate to rule-based guidelines through laziness or ignorance.

The easiest and poorest method of teaching anyone anything is to defer to rules, rather than take the time to actually evaluate and communicate intelligently—hence, teach.

The common cry when fixed rules are not followed by people who operate by using more common sense and individual reward/merit diversity with different people is the hue and cry that this is not equal treatment; it is favoritism, or it is even too productive and keeps other workers from finding work. These arguments are primarily sour grapes, and based more on envy and a poor understanding of how good working environments and teamwork are actually created.

Working with people through give-and-take, through measured responsibility and reward, is good for everyone, for overall morale and trust in any working environment. Just review the businesses that operate in this manner versus the businesses that operate based on friction through black-and-white operating conditions. The latter businesses are cold and wasteful and restrain the creative abilities of individuals. If any individual wants to contribute additional effort, then equal guidelines need to be applied.

Allowing freedom to workers is the ultimate equality.

This is also true in families with children, where guidelines for behavior are drawn. If you have one child who is exceptionally responsible and demonstrates great trust and worthiness, you can afford to bend the curfew and grant other little freedoms; however, if your other child is less trustworthy and pushes the limits consistently, you would not afford him or her any additional freedoms.

Equality means you treat people the same based on their behavior, not based on the guidelines for behavior. Those guidelines/rules will be used when you have abuses; then you enforce them with absolute commitment. But when responsibility begins to develop in someone, you move away from the use of fixed rules toward trust and common sense. This is the intangible medium of human potential that transcends mere rule-based methods of communication and actions.

This again is the essence of equality and fair treatment. You treat people the same by treating them differently, based on circumstance and/or behavior.

Do not expect the politically correct, or a bureaucrat, to have any understanding of any of this. They, by definition, do not respect values per se or common sense; they only respect control and condone actions, thoughtless or not, imposed on those who violate a particular set of written words (rules). Weak or artificial leadership simplistically respects operating from a point of high friction, operating from absolutes; as such, weak or artificial leaders are often demonstrated through zealot forms of behavior. They do not operate with common sense, as common sense implies following the intent of a law or rule, not always the letter of the law. Such reason would blur their fixed judgments and dismantle the self-righteous support pedestals that their identities are built upon. They do not understand the gray areas of communication, the merging of diverse views and opposite points of view to enable improved results. Such are the politically correct people who, on paper, appear to be social and corporate saints, but they are the first people who must be removed from positions of authority if optimized results and successes are to be realized.

Jack Welch, General Electric's former CEO and business author, has spoken of four types of workers: (1) the ones who make numbers and are part of the corporate culture, (2) those who make numbers but do not marry into the corporate culture, (3) those who do not meet numbers but meld well with the corporate culture, and (4) those who do not meet numbers and do not meet up with the culture. Number four types are easy to get rid of or remove from a business; number two types are critical to get rid of, but take the greatest effort and courage to do so. Number three types are good people and good people can always be turned around to make the numbers; but group number two, the people who make numbers, cannot always be made into good people.

This is what I believe Jack Welsh would argue. Jack Welsh is a true leader in the corporate world, which I would say only a handful of CEOs could lay true claim to. Richard Branson, CEO of Virgin Airlines, is another gentleman who is a true leader and a success in a brutally tough industry. He has spoken of not always hiring experts, but rather of hiring good people. Again, good people can become experts, but experts cannot necessarily become good people. This, in my view, echoes much of what Jack Welsh says.

I would add another corporate true hero of mine to the list of great CEOs: Herb Kelleher, former CEO of Southwest Airlines. Please read his book *NUTS*. Herb breaks the rules, trusts people—and wins. He is not what I would ever call politically correct; rather, he is genuine—a very rare commodity in this age. He is an icon and role model for all business leaders.

Another book that captures the essence of equality through different treatment based on behaviors as it outlines how to be a smart and effective manager is Ken Blanchard's *The One Minute Manager*. If you have not read that book, it is a great read. It is concise, capturing the essence of how to evaluate situations while teaming with and managing various types of people.

Finally, one of the greatest business leaders of our modern times is W. Edwards Deming, whose iconoclastic methods did not simply change a corporation, but changed a nation, Japan, into the quality center of the globe. In my view, Deming mirrored an understanding shared by John Wooden, the greatest coach in UCLA basketball history and a brilliant author, who believed in how amazing results can be accomplished if no one cares who gets the credit.

Dr. Deming was a world-class statistician, who was ironically fond of saying that "He that starts with statistical methods alone will not be here in three years as a business." His approach would also apply to athletics or any enterprise, as it is attitude and character that make a leader and a winner. Dr. Deming, like John Wooden and other unrivaled leaders, is intelligence and integrity personified, and they all stand out from the crowd. I would recommend any one of several books written about Dr. Deming, as he is an example of a consummate leader, not bound by conventional business practices. Dr. Deming honored the value of human beings by his lifelong commitment to excellence through a marriage of common-sense judgments and science. Dr. Deming's leadership methods led major businesses and the Wall Streets of the world, rather than being led by them and their conventional shortsighted quarterly analysts. Dr. Deming was the Einstein of business success, who certainly was not an unsung icon, but did not reach the sustained acclaim I believe he deserved. Frankly, he was flatly rejected by too many for some of his seemingly more unorthodox approaches to working with people, which were essential to his successful management formulas for business.

Other business leaders today, such as Warren Buffett and Bill Gates, are role models for common sense and demonstrate a caring for humanity that is lacking in our general business leadership today.

Great leaders with strong leadership qualities run short in this world, so be wisely skeptical and wary of charlatans, even though many of them are generally good people. I have found even the good folks are caught up in being first and foremost out for themselves. Then there are others who are simply not good people and are disguised in sheep's clothes. Their lip service is world-class. I also call them politically correct weasels. Foremost for leadership, measure all things against your standards, your ethics of high principles, and trust yourself first. Have character. By that I do not mean to demonstrate irreverence or disrespect for other people, but respectfully attempt to avoid being led by conventionalists and mere mediocrity. Find a way to influence and lead by example, an example that builds on cooperation rather than competition.

Let me try to capture this in brief poetic verse:

Truth is found between the lines, in the middle, where grays and paradox abound. It is found in give-and-take, through common sense—the law of shades. The engagement of truth is to be moral, rather than conventional, as egos can only scream in silence here.

For it is easier to be emotional, indignant, and anchored to the black or white than do the math. Truth's equations do dismantle aristocrats' might. Truth forever will scoundrels and ignoramuses frankly frighten.

Value your inner voice and find it, clarify it, use it. Your integrity requires it. The current state of the world can use you. Ignore the cries from the colorful demagogues, those who exploit and portray half-truths as facts to garner attention and promote self-serving agendas. In contrast to the demagogues, a true-hearted person lives in the middle, not in the extremes; is described and defined in character, not in cause; and is actually the person living in the peacemaker's seat, without grandiose identity—but with something more than flash and pomp. That person has honor, not medals; has kindness, not sentiment; has a respect for truth, not for agendas; and has a love for what is truly right, not for what is technically right. That is leadership.

If you find your inner voice, either quiet or overt, you will not become a politically correct nuisance to the world, creating volumes of unnecessary one-sided noise. You will become a much truer, more honest voice of diversity, merging the sounds and feelings of everyone through your voice, by your actions, in your symphony of thoughts, in your music that is intrinsic and somewhere in all of us.

That search for the *common denominator*—the common truth that resonates in us all—will never be found in the black-and-white sides of an issue or an organization, but in the middle, in the grays, between the lines, in the dance that brings us together. In that dance, both the magic and discipline of authentic ideals are born.

True effective leaders know this. They understand the dance: leadership is a melding of differences into one objective, and to accomplish that takes intelligence, which is sometimes reticent, sometimes overt, and sometimes a combination of both. You need to be straight and to know when to bend. The best of leadership is a combination of skills. But first and always foremost, it is built from a true individual, not a conventionalist. In other words, *character counts.* Integrity is essential. It is important to attract genuine respect from others. That respect translates into a bond and a trust that is essential and unmistakable. Think of the few who you can count on your hand who engender such respect and trust.

It is far too few.

Chapter 11

KILLING

Do no harm.
—Hippocratic Oath

When is it right to kill a human being? Is it ever right?

For me, capital punishment is never right in a civilized world.

However, it may be a pragmatic necessity in an uncivilized world. If you were living in primitive conditions without buildings to institutionalize people and were attempting to control brutal violence on a large scale, you would be in a different world than the one we live in on this planet at this time. Under such primitive, ruthless conditions, it might become a pragmatic necessity to kill someone if he or she were a threat to others and could not be incarcerated or controlled.

This is strictly a hypothetical situation, but if true, I would pragmatically have to choose the lesser of evils.

The general principle employed here is I would sacrifice the one for the many.

A before-the-fact killing:

If I had a one-week-old baby and I were told that if I killed the child, it would prevent the torturous deaths of a thousand human beings, I would kill the child. *One for the many* is the morality of choice for me, the pragmatic ideal I operate by to minimize harm or evil.

Another example: if I were told I had the ability to pull the trigger on a rifle fixed on a terrorist who was about to push the button to blow up a hotel with countless lives on the line, I would pull the trigger and kill.

Both of these examples are premeditated murder, and I would attempt to execute my killing without remorse.

After-the-fact killing:

If you asked me to kill someone "after the fact" from a previous event—such as if someone had murdered a group of innocent people in a brutal fashion—I would never condone the taking of the predator's life by execution. I believe, in every fiber of my being, that this is morally wrong. Simply to kill begets killing. This is vengeance, not justice, and therefore only perpetuates such behavior. Such capital executions are foremost a product of emotion and reaction, and hence based on the principles of indignant vengeance, not thoughtful or reasoned action. The latter comes of principled behaviors fostered by grace, wisdom, strength, and love. The former is fostered by selfishness, ill will, and indignation by way of emotional hate.

If we are to have a civilized world and promote its development and growth, as we do today, in a world with billions of people, we will have malfunctions of these people, whether physiological or psychological. These malfunctions or misjudgments will come from poor values or physiological or psychological defects. Knowing this reality, that a certain amount of statistical human failures are inevitable, socially we have an obligation to institutionalize these people, isolating them from the public in a civilized manner, rather than torturing them with acts of premeditated killing. Premeditated killing sends the wrong message to people looking for help or who are in need of help. If we took and actually loved these flawed and often vicious human beings, regardless of their behavior, they might actually change in the process.

The irony is not lost on me that many of our Christian leaders today believe in capital punishment; if they followed their leader Jesus, they could not abide such behavior. Again, the hypocrisy of these people is frightening, as in their adept selective reasoning, loss of logic, and loss of critical thinking, which seems anesthetized and replaced by the prurient and vindictive drugs of emotion, which vilifies and finds satisfaction in measuring their love for the loss of loved ones by demonstrating how well they can hate the perpetrators without remorse.

Hate begets hate; love begets love. We should fight the most negative situations in life with their opposites whenever possible. As we fight fire with water, we should fight hate with love.

Jesus did this, Gandhi did this, Dr. King did this. Why not us? Were these leaders not good role models? We do not fight a building on fire with hoses filled with fire; we use its opposite: water to cool the flames. So we should treat others, those who oppose us or who would do us harm or even kill us, ideally with opposite behavior. If we hate them, they will just continue to hate, but if we love them, they may eventually find respect for us, and change. This is the essence of doing onto others as you would have them do onto you. Loving your neighbor as you love yourself is *the Golden Rule.*

Unfortunately, many people believe that when a loved one is killed by a predator, the measure of their love for their lost one is somehow found in how well they can illustrate their vitriolic hate for the predator and call for the cruelest of punishments to be meted out.

I remember many years back when the Israeli legislative body, the Knesset, was working to reinstate a capital punishment law in response to a young person who was killed by a child molester. The crime was so unthinkable in their culture that it rallied the government to show its ultimate disdain for such heinous acts by working to reinstate the death penalty. At the same time, I saw the parents of the child who was molested and killed being interviewed about the current capital punishment law being passed for future crimes of that nature. The parents asked the government not to do this, saying that this was not what they or their child was about—such abject vengeance. It brought very unsentimental and valid tears to my eyes to listen to such loving people. This family was a model for everyone. They knew who they were in terms of principles, not in terms of emotions. If there is a God, they were manifesting God at that moment.

Many years ago I had a coworker a few years older than myself, a real gentleman. We were discussing the death penalty one night, and I told this person that if a drunk driver killed my spouse, I could not bring myself to wish that person additional harm. In my life, as in many millions of others, at some point I had driven drunk by legal standards, certainly in my youth, and just because I was fortunate enough not to have turned a blind corner and killed someone, I was certainly no different from someone who had done such a thing.

The quote that comes to mind in such a tragic situation is, "There but for fortune go you or I," or perhaps the religious version: "There but for the grace of God, go you or I." This is an irrefutable idea, which I think is lost to the unfortunate self-righteous in our societies today. I was explaining this point to that gentleman, and that ultimately, and ideally, I believed in compassion in virtually all such horrific situations.

He then proceeded to tell me that his young daughter had been killed by a teenage drunk driver in a hit-and-run on the front lawn of their house. Apparently the driver veered off the road and struck her. The young man was later caught and arrested.

At that moment, I thought to myself that I might have been too glib about how so many self-righteous people behave in such conditions.

Well, this gentleman brought deeply intimate, but reticent, tears to my eyes when he told me he and his wife decided not to let this tragedy be turned into something negative. They would work to live in a positive manner. They sought out the teenager who had killed their daughter in an accidental manner while driving drunk. They met him in jail and told him he had taken someone from them who was very talented and special, and denied their daughter her life, but at the same time, they told this young man that they forgave him. *That is love.* I had to look no further to find where true love lives than within the acts of this family. For some time after that, they continued to communicate with this young man. By the way, the man and his wife were Christians, and I would say they were the rare example of individuals who actually lived their faith. They were living examples of genuine *godly* values.

The Israeli couple and this other gentleman and his wife are the types of human beings the world is quite desperately in need of. I am awed by the presence of such loving human beings. They are all too rare.

I live in America, one of the beacons of freedom and liberty in the world. America has its failings, but it has a constitutional foundation and a Bill of Rights that speaks well of its goals and ideals, which are continuing to evolve—I hope for the better. Still, this great nation has a long history of supporting capital punishment, and worse, it seems the people living in this country, by an almost two-to-one margin, support capital punishment. That does not speak well for our leadership in the world, just as it does not speak well for our values.

Again, if we have human malfunctions, people who kill or maim and do harm to others, we, as a society, have an absolute obligation to humanely institutionalize these people in order to protect the public. Killing these people is equivalent to the behavior these misfortunate people exhibit. It is of the highest hypocrisy and thereby a disgrace that a free, generous, decent society would condone cruelty and vengeance as virtues by way of its jurisprudence and many of its religious institutions, leaders, and individuals.

Chapter 12

ECONOMICS (YIN/YANG)

The love of economy is the root of all virtue.
—George Bernard Shaw

I have heard the debate for my sixty-plus years on this planet regarding capitalism and socialism, and would be left adrift by the black-and-white absolutisms defining the characterizations of these two economic systems if it were not for my own presumptuous common sense. *Note:* I am not an economist, except for my own personal common sense—which many will no doubt object to!

I will be very economic (pithy) in this essay, comparatively speaking, based on my past ramblings: America is both capitalistic and socialistic within its approach to running economic policy. Neither economic position, neither capitalism nor socialism, is in and of itself a panacea for perfection. Both systems fail miserably when implemented as stand-alone economic policies.

America has chosen wisely to operate with the best of both economic philosophies as a hybrid of socialism (regulation) and capitalism. We have private enterprise and ownership, but regulated to allow for competition from the start-up's and small-ownership operations.

If any of you remember, when the J. P. Morgans and the Rockefellers nearly owned this country or complete industries, we had a situation that was true capitalism, whereby the most powerful could economically crush the small and the weak.

During the riotous times of establishing unions at the beginning of the twentieth century and with the help of the US Congress in the 1930s, we implemented regulations that subsidized the small businesses and rural landowners in order that they could be provided services—that is, telecommunications and other utilities—at rates far less than a free market would have allowed for. This regulated approach allowed for expansion and growth of so-called free markets within our great country. Free markets are a misnomer, as they only exist because they are subsidized by wealthier and more robust commercial operations, such as urban cities or highly consolidated industries produce.

In fact, when the old Ma Bell (telecommunications industry) said they would submit to regulation in the 1930s, it was thought to be capitalism heresy, but it helped create a country with universal communications and services not seen anywhere else in the world. By the way, this improved our national defense and overall security and fairness as a nation. As an example, it may have cost 10 million dollars to set up a communications switch in a rural town of only two hundred people, which could never afford to pay for such a communication system in a lifetime, but due to regulated monopolies being established that took greater revenues from the business and urban clients and used the money to support universal national communications, we succeeded, with a socialistic methodology tied hand in hand with capitalism.

In a pure capitalistic society, we would not have achieved the success we have produced and would still be a land of kings and paupers. In equal contrast, in a socialist economy, we would be a lazy, un-incentivized, mediocre society at best. It takes two to tango, and we did so by working with both economic models, those of capitalism and socialism, taking the best of both worlds and philosophies.

To live with belief systems that are only black and white, to believe one system or political party or economic philosophy is sacrosanct and always better than the other, is misguided and myopic thinking. We as a sound nation of sound values are a coalition of taking the best of all worlds, philosophies, and economics to find a stable, productive, and realistic world. It is not always fair, but fairness is the objective, never a fully satisfied end.

Pragmatism is the order of the wise, just as absolutist or black–and-white thinking is the order of ignorance and of the self-serving.

Thank goodness we took the path of common sense, and not ideology, through much of this country's improved growth and development.

Both our capitalism and socialism are what has made this country great economically. Even so, we are now faced with globalization, and that means consolidating our larger industries to become soundly and resolutely competitive abroad. This will put a wrinkle in our previous history's economic growth, but as long as we use both our heads and our hearts with liberty as our backbone, I hope we find the right mix of economic formulas to help lead the world to even better days of universal freedom and a fairer economic playing field for all.

If any of you reading this have an amplified view, I fully encourage you to enlighten me and others in amplifying both your knowledge of finance and your perspective. I certainly do not have all of the answers to fairness, which is probably a misnomer in a world that regularly feeds the strong off of the weak. But I can always hope we will work toward a better model for all.

The world is a project in motion. To believe that a single philosophy will be an end-all in an imperfect world is to hope for the impossible. Even though that is the utopian goal we should always work toward, ubiquitous fairness and utopia are not of this world. We should still never quit trying.

At any rate, we are a combination of economic practices in this great country, and to deny that is to be naïve, just as supporting any one single economic philosophy is just as equally naïve.

for the
teamwork
his new

Chapter 13

PARTISANSHIP

I have never seen such extreme partisanship, such bitter partisanship, and such forgetfulness of the fate of our fathers and of the Constitution.
—Robert Byrd

First, I would like you to know that I deplore and despise the labels of partisans.

But out of our language bag of restrictions, we often relate to the easiest form of communication, which is to use labels to simply identify a complex concept or tag an individual or group with a two-bit, easy label.

This, I believe, separates *us and ideas*, rather than *unifying* and *optimizing* potentials. In the same way, President George Washington believed that if the union regressed into parties, we would be less inclined to work for the common good, rather than our own self-oriented ends.

I agree with George. He believed it would hurt the union, and I believe it has too.

So with that explanation of labels and my disdain for them, let me define them at the same time, I hope with the point to demonstrate that we are really best defined and served well when we work together, rather than as partisans.

A conservative, in a general sense, is someone who wants to live by traditions of the past, whether right or wrong, and will go to often unrealistic extremes or far-fetched thinking to achieve their principles, or premises—such as fallaciously suggesting that science cannot prove that the earth has only been here for six thousand years. Sometimes this is, at its very core, born from past cultural and/or religious belief systems, which were construed before we had empirical scientific proofs or some reasonable scientific assumptions. Therefore, the shamans, or spiritual leaders, of the tribes would invent knowledge, based on hope, whim, dreams, and some wisdom, out of a controlling power methodology.

A liberal is someone who is open to almost any form of behavior, sometimes without any evaluation of risk or moral-related bounds. Morals are a touchy issue, as morals should, for me, be solely based on the Golden Rule and to "do no harm" when at all possible. But some liberals exceed this concept with a vengeance, but no more than conservatives, and adhere to their thinking with an *angry zeal*, which nullifies their principles or premise of open thinking. Certainly on a personal level, many people behave in this manner. Just watch them. Ironically, ego-based foolery too often is demonstrated by both conservatives and liberals!

In both labeled systems, watch for the groupthink behavior or individual behavior fraught with the fervor that they display by way of attitude or constructed language that bankrupts their integrity. When individuals do not retain the tenets of the Golden Rule and to "do no harm," observe the anger or even sometimes the depression and sociopathic listlessness driving their behaviors, which again, I repeat, demonstrates the folly and emptiness of the depth of their sincerity.

In conclusion, balance and common sense for both groups, I would argue, would bring them together, thus deposing their *label-based myopic pedestals* and reducing them as black-or-white label-made entities. Still, both so-called *conservative and liberal* labels do have some seminal values when viewed for selective merit. Certainly the traditions of history have taught us of our folly and improved us, just as forward thinking and openness too offer a view often ahead of their time. Most importantly, read between the lines and find the common ground—and evaluate behavior as equally as rhetoric.

Again, I personally deplore labels—hence my bias toward common sense or toward common ground and a belief that we can all work together without partisanship if we only give the subject matter being discussed *its true due. For example, when I see our US Congress vote along party lines, we experience a complete and utter failure to witness integrity. All we are seeing is groupthink and a miscarriage of justice toward the truth, toward peace, toward love, and toward right and goodness.*

When I witness such individual and groupthink behaviors, I am reminded of the word *pernicious*, which is one of the most eloquent words for the excesses that *label-driven or partisan people* demonstrate. Firmly the cant of hypocrisy is certainly on the move when partisanship is in play.

One final comment: Certainty it is obvious that we need labels to identify objects. Please grasp the gist of my theme here, as it is subject to the constraints of exposition afforded us via the limitations of language. *I am speaking about the labels of partisans, not objects.*

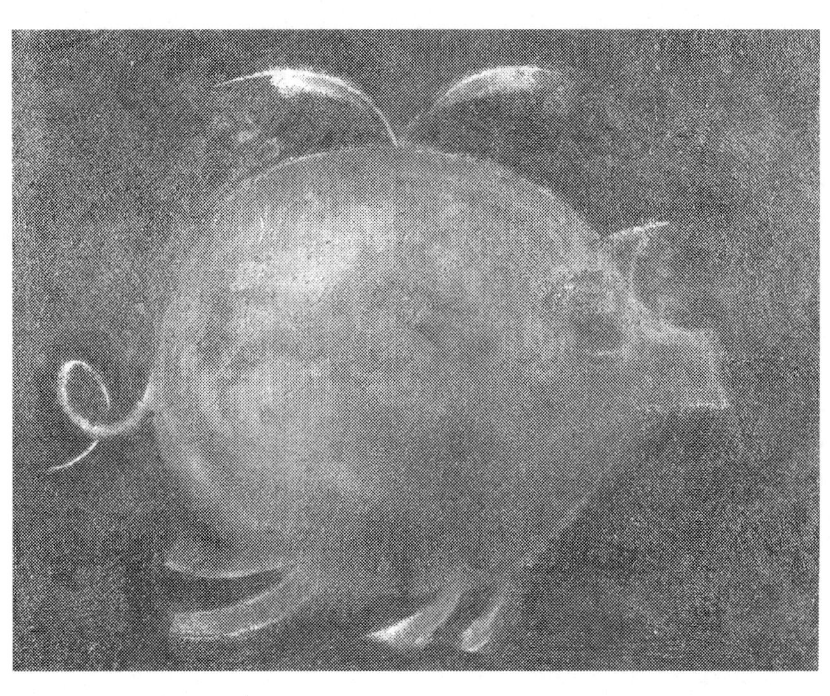

Chapter 14

POLITICS

Suppose you were an idiot and suppose you were a member of Congress . . . but I repeat myself.
—Mark Twain

You may have figured out my politics by now, but there's more to politics than a personal point of view. There is the nature of the beast itself, which this chapter addresses, as well as my own leanings.

Ideally politics should be the art of governing—a society, a community, or a world—with balance, moderation, and wisdom based on the principles of liberty and fair play.

Unfortunately, given that humans are not perfect, politics is also not perfect. As a result of our human flaws of insecurity, ego, and selfish interest, societies manifest *partisan politics.*

It is ironic that our liberties are controlled or manifested upon the Machiavellian power plays and the hyperbole of political opponents.

You would believe, based on much of our political parties' behaviors, that each party operates as a monarchy, as despots, in absolute conflict and with a continuous effort to disable the other party. *This is true not all of the time, but too much of the time.* Welcome to partisan politics.

Ultimately, however, general compromise or simple voting blocs win the day, and we avoid implosion—such as with a civil war—but we do not necessarily get good government. Certainly in the news you see personal matters impacting a political figure on a regular basis. You can almost be assured someone from the other party is attempting to gain political mileage out of those personal and private family issues. I understand that private lives involve character and have relevance, but balanced respect for decency seems often abandoned within the political arena. This shameful behavior by so-called leaders is given credence by too many.

Partisan politics is an obstruction to good government. I have never registered in a political party because I have never supported *us and them* labels. Pragmatically, if I ever ran for a political office, I would, by necessity, have to join the two-party majority system and which party I chose would be a momentary decision based on practicalities. I consider myself neither liberal nor conservative. I consider myself down the middle, which encompasses both conservative and liberal attributes depending on the circumstance. I support principles that are linked to a given objective, with exception to partisan politics that logroll and find value in political gamesmanship and shameful underhanded political vendettas.

In general, I find that politicians exemplify partisanship, not statesmanship. Statesmanship acts and thinks both *with the people* and *for the people* in a manner that works for the benefit of all. Partisans act in lockstep with their team label of Democrat or Republican, to name two, for example, to advance advantage over their opponent, not to advance leadership or effective legislation, but to advance political gamesmanship to advantage their political party's base in the end. Statesmanship seizes on understanding, cooperation, and integration. Partisanship seizes on self-interest, meanness, and segregation.

Since our representatives are regionally based politically, they have the proclivity to engage in what US House of Representatives Tip O'Neil captured perfectly: "All politics is local." In other words, self-interest becomes the order of the day, whether for your region or your political party. This should not be.

The impacts of this reality are corrupting good government.

To avoid this intrinsic failure in the nature of the political process of good government, you need leaders who are not party loyalists, but individuals first and foremost. You need leaders who are centered on uniting, not dividing, which is personified by partisan politics.

As a young man, my friends told me I should be a Democrat. The older I became, the more often they told me I should be a Republican. I have a real disdain for labels and political-party parlor politics that cause separation, not cooperation. My agenda or politic is not based on party but on policy, as I think many people tend to agree with, whether registered to a political party or not.

The country in which I live, America, has a tradition that changed the last couple of centuries on this planet. It offered liberty and freedom to people fleeing various tyrannies, both economic and social. America's foundational ideal is my politic. The current two-party political system is simply the structure that attempts to execute America's founding ideals. Those structures have become organized self-serving entities unto themselves, whose sometimes first allegiance is to their own party's survival, not to America's. Simply stated, the party is more important than the country when partisan politics is in play.

Perhaps the two-party system is the best we can devise to run a democracy or republic, but it is a system of snares and pitfalls that requires honest review and statesmanship to run it well.

Certainly as you review history, the wax and wane of policies between the two parties is obscure. For instance, President Bill Clinton had the statesmanship to contain spending and implement work for welfare. People misguidedly assumed such goals were Republican goals, but President Bill Clinton knew they were pragmatic balanced objectives not respective of party. President Bill Clinton accomplished some sound objectives that are generically good, not Republican or Democrat. Additionally, traditional big spending is assumed to be a Democrat trait, but President Clinton was, by and large, fiscally responsible. Actually, President Ronald Reagan and President George

W. Bush, along with President Barack Obama were the biggest spenders of all time. To be fair, while Congress authorizes spending, it is the executive branch that authors and submits the budget. Ronald Reagan, George W. Bush and Barack Obama appear to be nearly purists when it comes to Keynesian economics at nearly full throttle, a Democrat trait by assumption. A Democrat today, one might believe, could scarcely get away with such loose spending policies and survive. However, President Obama, has broken that mold, as peculiar economic times may turn the tables on us all, once again showing the ebb and flow of changes between policy changes of Republicans and Democrats.

Other inverse examples of party distinctions are the anti-Communist Nixon took us to China, and the progressive Lincoln was a Republican; the list goes on. Parties wear different policy hats dependent on other affiliations and the times, which demonstrate the obscure differences in the flavors of party identities. Which party is progressive and which is traditional continues to morph and change.

In truth, the obfuscation of principles between these political parties' wary distinctions is a good thing as it builds on their more nuanced diversities to a single objective of working for and with the people together, rather than for their party's deluded notion of a *better-than-you* syndrome, which is regressive and fallacious. Such partisan behavior and perspectives are destructive to good government, as you may note from my previous chapter about partisanship.

Clearly good ideas are not Republican or Democrat; they are practicalities of the moment, gifts, and manifest out of fortunate events that good sense and reason should seize upon. Both parties do this when operating well. The parties are at their best when collaborating and working *for and with* the people in a check-and-balance mechanism of ideas, not as an us-and-them, black-and-white team sport.

As I see the political parties today, and with few exceptions, over my lifetime, I see partisan theater, melodramatic/demagogic elucidations of the issues, and highly superficial respect for the other side of the aisle. The cliché-driven oratory and grandstanding is juvenile and poor theater. The differences between the two parties are more nuanced, albeit some important nuances, but both parties seem to abide by their hierarchy's party line, regardless of constituency, reason, or integrity. Party lines are *tired old hoodwinking rhetoric* about how "good we are" and about how "bad they are." They appeal to the selfish in us, rather than the selfless.

With some notable and encouraging exceptions, my view of the current-day leadership of the parties is that they are too often weak and fumbling, almost substantively anemic, while attempting to appease every interest group. Democrats are famous for the so-called *leftist* issues, but they now hold to fiscal belt-tightening, while the Republicans are offering spending for all, along with baseline support for the religious so-called *rightist* issues.

As of originally writing of this book, the current Democrats have some leaders who have few legislative accomplishments of note, nor do they seem to represent much more than political lapdogs, touting tired old clichés of justice and gifts to all. Substantive anemia is sometimes probably too weak a description. They disappoint me, but no less than the Republicans. The Democrats' rhetoric of principles from some of the leadership, not necessarily the rank and file, has become almost demagogic utopianism. They need some new leaders who are not just sugar-and-spice-and-everything nice.

The failure of neoliberalism (neolib) is that it does not acknowledge the selfish underbelly of humanity, that once you offer assistance, some will take advantage. They need not cast pearls before swine, nor act the demagogue in offering what they have no prescription to deliver.

The neo-republicans (neocons) are equally uninspiring and misguided in their overzealous current-day interventionist policies abroad. We are breaking at home and need to work here foremost—*and that means supporting the world, too, by the way.* We are truly a wealthy nation, both in economics and values, and should be a generous nation, providing not only our wealth but leadership. But security and leadership begin at home, and I would argue, *even in light of a new era of increased global economic and social interdependence, which we ignore at our own peril*, that we are breaking the balance between the two priorities of internal and external interests. I will agree that internal and external interests are becoming one and the same, but how we manage those must be done in a manner that is sometimes subtle, even covert, sometimes overt and aggressive. Again, I think the neocons are on a current one-speed-ahead aggressive path that does not serve their well-intended interests for us or the world. Republicans, like the Democrats, act the role of demagogues in offering what they also have no sound prescription to deliver.

At the time of the writing of this book, the disappointment with the Republicans as of late is they slightly have, more than the Democrats, demonstrated the courage of conviction to state economic and social realities. *Ronald Reagan was a good example*, but Ronald Reagan had scarcely an iota of courage to act on his rhetoric of economic principle—he never authored a balanced budget. Tragically, though, with exception, the Republicans have intervened in areas in which I categorically disagree, namely on the social front, where their neo-conservative positions on religion and lack of patient/individual rights issues are anything but *limited—government-and-liberty-based.* It is as if they are, in many ways, the neo-inquisition-fundamentalists for faith-based intrusion into personal lives, the new champions of big government versus individual liberty and the values of limited government. Clearly the Democrats are not without some of these same ideologues as well.

For me it is hard to get a fix on either party's core values when both parties' modus operandi when on the political-speaking stump is too often built upon bravado, innuendo, and aspersion rather than facts, reason, and collaboration.

The reality for me is that these two parties will eventually, perhaps within an administration or two, actually flip-flop on the issues as I have described them in current terms—perhaps not entirely, but to some degree. Our two-party system's notion of substantive difference is more opaque than clear. What is different about these groups is that each party is vying for power over the other through appealing to some very different competing special interests. These special-interest groups are, foremost, self-serving, not necessarily for our liberties and common interests, but for their niche organizational goals. *I would note that some special-interest groups do have more than organizational self-interest at stake, just as some of the business, social, or environmental agendas may have sound merit.* Still, the special interests in this country own the dollars behind political parties, when it would be far better to have a true statesman rally these sometimes disparate groups to work together. I would somewhat argue that party differences are certainly over time obscure, and they are built primarily on the backbone of an us-and-them structural nature. That structural nature is, unfortunately, more about the power of self-interest than the power of liberty, for which this country of America was founded.

I believe nearly everyone would agree it is better when we come together in a cause for liberty and justice, rather than obscure and dilute our common cause through us-and-them politics, or in other words, *partisan politics.*

As a solution, both parties should routinely revisit their roots and the realities of the day, and tether their leanings to true libertarianism, from which both parties originally sprang as they opposed the governments of previous monarchies. Not that libertarianism *in and of itself* is the answer, since I also realize it, too, is somewhat utopian. However, it has great fundamentals we should aspire to: individual liberty and limited government.

That is where I am with my politics—and why I still have chosen not to join any one party.

I am very much anti-nationalistic, as I see nationalistic behavior as a dangerous black-and-white idea of "I'm better than you are," bravado pedestal to be standing on. Good is good; it is not nationalistic or specific to any particular political party. Goodness and sound humane values thrive best when their examples speak for them, not when they pound their chests and disparage others. Humility is the essential key to success here.

Too often Democrats and Republicans are so wrapped up in themselves and their parties, they forget about America or the bigger picture of humanity in general. Partisan politics is the death of leadership and a stumbling block to the ideals America stands for.

It is my understanding that George Washington, the first president of the United States, never believed in the value of political parties. Rather, I suppose, we should have candidates' debate and then make our ballot-box choices. This may be structurally naïve, but it is a position that has solid benefits as well. It is where I would prefer to see us work from, since the partisanship of our day seems so often self-defeating to America's enunciated ideals. I would propose we all run for office under our personal platforms in a primary and then in a general election and have a runoff between the two leading candidates. Legislative committee leadership would work in a similar fashion. But then again, this will never happen with the traditions we have virtually enshrined, and it possibly lacks the needed financial reality that political parties supply. However, I think the question is worthy of debate to promote better cooperation, versus competition, within the political process.

Today, our two-party system is much too controlled by the edge groups—neolibs and neocons—and as a result, we are precariously too ideological. Both groups see mecca at the end of their ideological rainbow, but neglect the practical matters necessary regarding the journey to actually get there. That journey is more pragmatic and proposes balance and review based on circumstances. That journey is sometimes liberal and sometimes conservative. This balanced point of view, this sense of *statesman-like reason,* is lacking in polarized political leadership, and I would add from the public masses, who demagogue with the best of them as well, which often is too partial toward its political party's platform. Fortunately, the process of democracy intervenes, and we are forced to review the ideological rhetoric from these polarized bodies. This forced review of the pontificating political mix of ideological melodramas, in the end, comes to an often more practical and balanced solution—but not always. When statesmanship is lacking in our leadership, then the democratic process is far too protracted, resulting in our failure to act in an effective, timely manner. It is critical to note that our new *high-speed* technological era has exponentially changed the playing field of ideas and solutions and the importance of how they are executed in timely manners. Technology waits for no one, and we need to recognize the equivalent necessity of swift and thoughtful, less-protracted political solutions. Either we lead, or we, as a people and a nation, will be led by technology as second-fiddle minstrels to the orchestrated tunes no longer within our control.

The moral of the story is that we can afford to improve and should find the humility and good sense to do so. We need greater *balance and reason*, not *us-and-them* processes, dominating the political groups running our country or any enterprise in today's world, from family to business to governments.

Partisanship needs to take a sedative and rest for the future good of everyone—except the political talking heads, as they might be largely out of work if the ideological mentalities wane, giving way to responsibility.

I also would add the politics of segregation in any form other than perhaps humor, lighthearted camaraderie, and sport, or for specific short-term social goals, is a tricky minefield. Organizations and groups, be they nationalists, businesses, racial, ethnic, religious, political, or even social—often have a proclivity to unite themselves as a group, but divide themselves from and against others to a fault. This so-called diversity can sometimes become more divisive than uniting. It needs to be reasoned out and managed with diligence. We should be building a united front in this life, not a divided one, not one of us-and-them.

In resting my case on this subject, I am going to focus on two quotes. The first quote is humorous but much too true.

A lot has been said about politics; some of it complimentary, but most of it accurate.
—Eric Idle

The quote above illustrates the politically indigenous proclivity that "all politics are local." This conventional slide away from integrity into a tangled web many politicians weave to suit a moment's convenience and self-interest binds and captures too many good individuals to the detriment of all.

Finally is a quote from a politician with some genuine boundless statesmanship, *at times*, but as time went by in his political career, it looked as if the web of the partisan political weavers was beginning to trap him as well. Nonetheless, this quote stands on its own for the ages. We should continue to take note of such truisms in order to hold at bay those temptations that limit our integrity, and always direct ourselves to continue to grow and avoid the stagnation of accepting what we could otherwise make better.

Conformity is the jailer of freedom and the enemy of growth.
—John F. Kennedy

Make no mistake from my comments about America and its politics. While I believe thoughtfulness and improvement are incumbent upon us to sustain success, we live in the greatest and most successful political experience of the ages.

Chapter 15

It Only Takes One Thing

We have committed the Golden Rule to memory; let us now commit it to life.
—Edwin Markham

What a world it is—what a world it could be . . .
It only takes one thing: the Golden Rule.

The Golden Rule is ethics. It stands irrefutably, indelibly, and infinitely on its own, devoid of the need for support from culture, religion, or politics.

It is agnostic, theist, and antitheist seamlessly strung together in perfect sympathetic union, as it is no respecter of personal dogmas. As such, the Golden Rule is ethics personified, the common denominator that merges diversity into unified form, the true ether of sentient conscience.

Nobel Prize laureate Albert Camus said, "Integrity has no need of rules." I understand the ethical intent of his point when based on the Golden Rule. But to be even more precise, I would say, "Integrity of ethics has no need of rules."

What a world that would be.

The reason I added the word *ethics* in the quote above is that the derivation of *integrity* comes from the Latin meaning *individual.* The inference is that an individual is not subject to changeable fair-weather conventional thinking but is first and foremost independent and therefore can be trusted, simply because social conditions will not change a true individual. But clearly, individuals can be trusted to be either good or bad based on ethics. In contrast, social conditions will often change a person who lacks integrity, whose beliefs and behaviors are based on outside sources, fads, whims, or cultural, religious, or political dogmas. Hence, integrity and ethics must be in union to effect goodness and disband the need of rules. As George Bernard Shaw would have stated it, "People are not moral, merely conventional." An individual or someone with integrity can be trusted, as in contrast, a conventional person would be less reliable. Hence, people's ethics would be respective of their conventional or individual (integrity-based) dispositions.

Clearly as a result of the importance of integrity and an understanding of the issues I will explain in the following paragraphs, the only moral absolute or ethic I can with logic envision is the Golden Rule, as that is a principle based on circumstance or context, rather than fixed dogma.

I believe that integrity and the Golden Rule are in lockstep in order for sincere virtue to manifest itself. They are the embodiment of our core ethical or spiritual teachings central to our most decent and altruistic leaders throughout history, coupled with the personal nature of sentient knowledge within our stand-alone individual selves.

All other moral absolutes that are written as one-dimensional concepts, such as "Thou shall not lie," are based on strict un-equivocating and unyielding adherence to a principle, a rule, or law. Such absolute concepts that ignore the value of context or the variables and nuances of actions or circumstances all fail to define the true facts of actions or events, with results that derail the presence of truth and promotion of human dignity. For instance, the premise of "Do not kill" is a moral absolute; however, I believe pragmatically that killing may become the lesser of two evils, if killing one person could save millions of lives. In this example, I must out of moral duty relinquish my moral position of not killing someone for the good of the many. This type of killing is not born out of the vices of revenge or selfish motives but out of charity and kindness. Such actions are only executed out of the fundamental notion of the Golden Rule.

A simple example of this type of moral action would be if I were a pacifist but was told that I had the opportunity, without any other options, to pull the trigger on a rifle that was fixed on a terrorist who was only seconds away from pushing the button to blow up a hotel with a thousand innocent lives in the balance, I would have to pull the trigger and kill.

As a result of the example above, I am in practice executing the principle of the one for the many, while at the same time I am sacrificing my pacifist absolutism. This is an act of pragmatic judgment, incumbent upon ethical sentient beings. Therefore, any personal, cultural, or religious opposition to this ethical position should be discarded from all human discourse.

This position does not sit well with those who operate by way of singular rigid positions, suggesting that honor is honor or the law is the law, without the notion of give-and-take. In other words, absolutes are unequivocally absolutes—or in the vernacular of our current day, zero tolerance is commonly stated as the only acceptable approach to address a particular situation.

Well, I would say both yes and no, depending on context, to such absolutes and self-righteous moral rhetoric. That is the fundamental reality and conundrum that language seems to confine us to—yes or no, either/or, and black or white—seemingly fixed positions, but only if we allow it to be so. Ideally, we must make judgments about our moral positions that sometimes conflict with our so-called moral positions in order to truly be moral. In other words, to stand pure to a belief that restricts pragmatism and the exercise of human judgment is to relegate humanity to being no more than thoughtless drones, devoid of integrity or virtue. Virtue is self-sacrifice, even the sacrifice of moral conviction if it means that the outcome will benefit goodness in the end.

With our basic common sense, we know an honest person and a dishonest person, a loving action and an unloving action. Sometimes both decent and deplorable actions require guile and disguise; sometimes they require humility and raw truth from our behavior to secure decent results. White lies and lies are actually different, but again, that does not sit well with a moral absolutist, whose honor is based on a strict code of one-sided conduct. Hence, "thou shall not lie." This type of moral absolute position is fatal to the ultimate premise of decency, given the fact that there are distinctions in the function and purpose of a lie. It's that simple. For instance, some lies can ameliorate the unnecessary harshness of facts that would unnecessarily make someone who is emotionally ill even more despondent and potentially cause him or her to harm himself or herself or others or even to commit suicide. This type of lie is no less a lie, but its intention is kind and moral.

However, what happens when you try to convince the politically correct, a true red-blooded, brain-dead bureaucrat, or someone with deep personal, cultural, or religious absolutist-zealot tendencies of this type of measured judgment and decency that must be applied to human thought and action? Often very little. But we all, I believe, should continue to try, because without uplifting the education of the world to thinking critically in the moment, rather than relying on the traditions of the past, we very well may condemn and destroy all of us, and at the very least will indirectly cause harm to the many innocent who are killed by fanatics through our otherwise inaction.

We all see it today with suicide bombers, maiming and destroying in the name of Allah, and we have seen it in the past centuries as well from various religious and secular structures. But in the past there was one grave difference: there were no weapons of mass destruction. Give it some thought.

And give this quote from Socrates some thought as well: "The only good is knowledge, and the only evil is ignorance."

The current ignorance that is so endemic in our global social fabric is born from the past abuses of power and from mankind's early mythologies and superstitions, used as poor substitutes for knowledge and science to make sense of the fundamental unknowns of our universe. In today's world, such ancient early foundations for truth and knowledge continue to dismantle goodness by way of such ignorance. Tragically, with a world of new technologies that contain weapons of mass destruction, it only takes one individual (one bit of ignorance) to harm us all.

Technology has changed the balance of power.

It is no longer an advantage for an aristocrat or a king or queen and the powerful and mighty of this world to indulge in keeping the masses ignorant or pacified in order to manage with hopeful and wishful calm. Ignorance today has within its control the power of the mighty and powerful of yesterday but with less to lose. So the ignorant of today will commit to mutual destruction, unlike those of the past, whose knowledge, wealth, and means kept them relatively less committed to mutual destruction.

Such absolutists and bureaucratic policy-fixed thinkers, or in other words, rigid thinkers, that do not value the context of an action are the province of many groups, such as the politically correct, often the naïve or immature, or secular and religious fundamentalists who will rally an issue to an extreme, whereby all rationale is lost.

It is also important to recognize that, conversely and ironically, however, absolutists are sometimes equally honorable sincere people, too, who simply hold to altruistic goodness.

As such, we live in a confounded world of paradoxes. Language (words) keeps us consorting with all sorts of strange bedfellows (people and principles), seemingly defined by the same terms when we communicate with one another. This very truth, this reality, is a vivid and insidious contrast for the wise to understand and for the unwise and selfish to demagogue about, through rant or rage ad nauseam, to the ultimate destruction of moral ethos.

So how do we get a handle on this diverse melting pot of contention between adversaries or philosophical opponents? Well, we may never. But that does not mean we should not continue to try. In other words, apply the ethic of the Golden Rule when confronted with an obstacle, a dilemma, and a conundrum. Think about how you would operate if held to that standard, the standard of wanting to be treated with altruism, with goodness, with understanding first and foremost. Then proceed with your judgment, hopefully understanding that is then manifest at that point in your analysis, and thus your behavior.

Understand that either virtuous or infamous principles are not always black and white. Common sense and sound, pragmatic action sometimes require behaviors or actions that are nuanced or mitigated, not absolute. While absolute principles such as love and hate are fundamentally black and white positions, they require the common denominator of reason to measure how we apply them to a given situation.

Simply seek out and find companions in this world who understand life, not the ones who judge it, and you will find the infinite, indefinable essence of goodness and justice within humanity. Know that words cannot always do justice in defining justice. Perception and actions combined are the purest measure of a decent person, of justice itself.

As you look to the law and written values to define behavior, look to the nature and constructs of balance that have been added to law, such as the principle of jury nullification or the doctrine of equivalents within patent law, as well as other balanced mechanisms that attempt to arbitrate law through judgment, not through cultural, moral, or technical rule-based absolutes. These constructs, such as jury nullification or the doctrine of equivalents, allow for the superseding of the rule of law to be subordinated by the arbitration of duly appointed arbiters, should fairness and justice be better served. In other words, the law ideally is written to be addressed when the intent of the law is violated, not the letter of the law. To determine this distinction requires one to arbitrate wisely, hence, use balanced judgment and nothing less if you expect the law to emulate fairness and truth. Law based on rules only is harmfully shallow, empty, and wanting when justice is the goal.

Differently said, balance is the key to success in all things, not commitment for the sake of commitment and adherence to technicality. That is the road to war, not to union, not to productive communication, not to understanding, and not to *humility*—that bears all things decent. In other words, laws and rules, in their wisest application, are used as guidelines that hold to the intent of the law or rule, rather than to the technical letter of the law or rule.

We as a species are so much more than the sum of our words; we are the sum of our understanding, which stretches beyond the confines of mere words. Words by themselves are a finite vehicle that have lent themselves both to good ethical behavior and to artfully and shamefully pandering in the name of truth through demagoguery or cultural and ideological paradigms. Simply because something sounds good or obvious, or traditionally true, does not make it so.

Do not let words wrap you up into one-dimensional boxes. Words often have far more to express through a broader understanding of their definitions than by holding onto a myopic view of what a word or words singularly and theoretically appear to mean. Words are often multidimensional, not one-dimensional. For example, it is often brought up in religious or theological conversations that truth is either fixed or it is relative.

I would argue that truth is both fixed and relativistic; the two are not mutually exclusive. What is true yesterday and today is also true tomorrow. But that truth is based on how a set of circumstances impact an event. (Please refer to the examples above regarding "Thou shall not kill" or "Thou shall not lie," and yet someone may be required to accomplish the pragmatic fundamentals of the Golden Rule by breaking those commandments.)

My point is that words can tie us up into illogical knots, and as such, unethical behavior, if we allow them to. Words are tools, not fixed absolutes. When we use the often one-dimensional notion of words as a truth descriptor to try and describe situations that are actually multidimensional when viewed within context, we do an injustice to the actual event or situation being described. Words at their best are actually multidimensional when we apply measured judgment and reason and understand the full context of a situation. The truth is that words are not the thing (situation/event) described; words only represent. (This is fundamental to understand.) Unambiguously we must be wise in our application of words and the weighted values we afford them if we are to judge accurately and fairly in this life.

The nature of words (etymology) is both precise and imprecise, based upon an individual's perceptions, and this variability will bear both fairly and unfairly on the truth. Certainly words are society's organizational tools and certainly the tools of any decent social structures' foundation in law. The wrinkle in this reality is that the facts of law and the necessary understanding of words are often variable in both intent and meaning.

This variability of words has become the law's and lawyers' tools, as they try to define contexts and circumstances underpinning a behavior or action. Sometimes lawyers use words to tie truth up into a fixed, seemingly immutable, box, while their counterpart may argue with the same words but with different frames of reference to clarify their perceived truth and expand that same so-called immutable box of facts.

Again, words are not the truth; only events are the truth. And to understand events, we must use words to communicate, but balanced with the mathematics of human intellect, based on objective values founded by the Golden Rule, to effect justice in order to actually experience and know truth.

Jurisprudence in its highest and most noble of forms understands this principle behind the specter and shadow cast by the circumscribed nature of words. Hence, the notion and beauty of arbitration emerges, which attempts to bridge this breech between the words of the believed-obvious (perception) and actual balance of reality. Arbitration is our ultimate means of delivering thoughtful and proper justice. Ironically, arbitration can be used through words to deliver the opposite result as well. But I would defer to educated, objectively trained arbiters and intellects—for lack of better terms, I suppose—before I would defer to traditional rules or the dogmas administered by ideologues in all matters of value and objective truth whenever we use words as our truth seekers or descriptors of unbiased cultural humane values.

This is the foundation of the Golden Rule and why integrity, not conventionalism or tradition, is incumbent upon every individual to personally define and operate by, as long as it is premised on the Golden Rule. Traditions are invaluable, but they are only hopefully sound building blocks for behaviors, not always ultimate panaceas.

We are the actions of the sum of our parts, of our histories and traditions. Ideally those actions produce goodness through the Golden Rule, rather than the selfish gain that has been often bred through the so-called goodness of ideologues', religions', or cultures' behavioral absolutes. You do not need culture or religion to operate by the integrity of the Golden Rule. There is no other conscious constant in the universe to live by—if you choose to be decent and loving—beyond this single and humble truth called the Golden Rule, which all sentient beings are knowledgably endowed with. If you believe anything of Maslow's studies of human motivational hierarchy, then at a survival level, perhaps many humans behave as selfish animals, but at the higher modes of psychological functions, we are enabled quite consciously with the humanity of the Golden Rule.

All great decent leaders in history and current times lived by this non-hate, non-warring notion, whether of ancient past great religious names or of our contemporaries, such as the current Dalai Lama or Gandhi or Dr. Martin Luther King. We would do well to follow such ancient or contemporary leaders in their wisest moments by way of their loving altruism. To do so would be to follow and embrace the truth of decency, genuine generosity, rather than selfish-centered judgment, and thereby manifest genuine goodness, rather than political correctness or static ideological fundamentalism disguised as goodness.

To follow any other edict in life beyond the Golden Rule such that would do unnecessary harm to others is to follow evil and unnecessary destruction, which will never enable you to embrace the sincerity and holiness of truth or the power of forgiveness and goodness.

In other words, we as a world community need to commit to goodness, not destruction, not to dictators or religious ideologues nor to ancient, perhaps well-meaning cultural traditions, but rather first and foremost, we need to commit to ourselves to care for others, rather than harm them—to find our integrity in order to do right. There is no other way to be sincerely kind or decent. All who will tell you that there is another way are wrong, perhaps well-intended, but wrong.

Again, as I think of the great and decent loving leaders from our history and those from our current times—and you all know their names—who embodied love for others by turning their cheek or insisting on goodwill toward others, they first and foremost were not slaves to the leadership of their contemporaries' foolish, selfish, or destructive dogmas. In fact, some of these leaders were thought to be heretics by the secular and religious establishments in their own times due to the fact that they were leaders who broke with convention as they implicitly and foremost operated with their integrity by way of the Golden Rule.

Hence, if we lived by their guidelines, we would no longer be the hypocrites we are or harm others in the name of God, Allah, religion, culture, politics, or tradition.

What a world that would be.

It only takes one thing.

LE
OV

Chapter 16

The Whole Bowl of Cosmic Soup

Love will keep us alive.
—Jim Capaldi

In considering how I really see the world, the good of the world and the misuse of that good, I have come to believe—or at least hope with some evidence and a lot of faith—that we evolve toward being a planet of human beings who follow some of my mother's living maxims: *to live and let live*, and *to make the best of things*, regardless of circumstances. Think about those two maxims. In the end, if we do these things, we ultimately will be honest with ourselves and with others, and we will genuinely begin to *love* more than we do today. And that is what the world really needs, however cliché.

Your goal should be to love others as yourself, to live by values that take patience and discipline, rather than react to events, as simple amoebas do. Whenever we begin to actually take stock of real human qualities, rather than squander those qualities through the vices of self-absorbed unloving hate, vengeance, and ill will toward our fellow human beings, we will begin to be a light unto others—and have some value. Until then we are nothing but an unnecessary nuisance, useless noise, troublemakers, and the ignorant pawns demagogues will continue to use to run this world.

Situations in our everyday lives are a *sometimes-and-sometimes* event. Our lives and the daily events we participate in are subject to a myriad of circumstances that we can give our distinct and due judgments to, or respond with the scapegoats, and for some, the accepted dictates of an ideologue's pronouncements. The choice is a human one.

I have said it before: "To achieve justice takes more than the rule of law; it requires human judgment." The rule of law, founded in humane principles, is the bedrock of a free and decent society. However, the rule of law is a mere tool of the people, which must be permeable and subordinate to the people; it should never be held sacrosanct. Human reason based on context must sometimes trump the rule of law for the sake of justice. The rule of law, while critically important as a social guideline, can be, in some instances, a crude, mechanical, and inappropriate application of justice. Justice, while based in a set of rudimentary dogma, is actualized only through the prism of reason, understanding, and wisdom.

If we fail at our attempts to exercise our unique human abilities to evaluate and use reasoned judgment based on events, devoid of ideology or inflexible rules, we will have failed doing right by ourselves and the human race, by giving into the ease of social conventions, the ease of emotional comforts, and ignorance. Morality requires not convention, but integrity. Human beings must communicate, exchange, and find common foundations from which to judge. However, if that judgment is built upon anything but humane reason and the science of the world as it progresses, then it is based upon the sands of self-deception and wishful thinking, and is failing itself and everyone it leads.

I am finishing this first part of the book with a very powerful and positive subject. This is a subject involving one of the greatest physicians, educators, and friends any one of us can have. And that panacea is humor.

Never let it go; never let the bureaucrats, politically correct, fundamentalists, or fuddy-duddies take it away. Humor is freedom. As with all things, an aspect of humor can also be cruel if inflicted onto innocents for the purpose of hurt or used for demagogically driven agendas, but short of those unkind or selfish ends, it is nirvana and heaven in living form. One could argue that it is the essence of our cosmic soup itself.

I once heard Alan Watts, a former preacher and a philosopher in later years, quizzically share a point about God and the angels in both a humorous and profound notion. *Take this, a paraphrase, for what it is worth:*

The reason angels can fly is that they take themselves lightly. And so, how much truer of God is that? In other words, symbolically God reflects consummate lightness and *humor; hence, the close alignment of the word humanity itself.* Nonsensical joy and humor become God, rather than the deep, dark, brooding wrath that has been propagated through pulpits fostering solemn admonitions, spewing woes to those who sin, with all the overburdened weight, serious guilt, and eternal damnation that a God would heap upon them.

Humor, silliness, and joy, among other wonderfully uplifting adjectives and nouns, have, at minimum, the equivalent depth and value as serious issues. I do not know if love begets humor or humor begets love. I guess it is as fundamental a question as the chicken and the egg. What I do believe is that once people touch the fruitless image-riddled notion of stern maturity and find it wanting, as they find charlatans abide in such serious postures, they come to know the value of humor and the balance it sets in motion, turning the tables on the facades of the truly superficial and sentimental or so-called serious and mature.

Humor, in its best sense, compels humility, integrity, and wisdom. And perhaps it ignites in us a touch of more than what we fully know. Perhaps, as Alan Watts intimates, humor is the personification of God itself. I want to leave you with both a succinct and appropriately paradoxical thought. Also, as conundrums go, it possesses its own humor. This poetic phrase, I think, sums up our greatest value. Give it a ponder.

No one wins in love
Love but wins itself.

Poetic Prose

(Break Time)

Across Space and Time

To really love is to meet without desire, without pretense, within common goals directed outside the passions of personal attraction.

So that personal desires are not the initial impetus,
but rather secondary blossoms of the vine.

Wherein the initial nature, character, principle, and
common atmosphere in which you met is not overridden
or altered in a vain pining effort to please.

Albeit to please is the truest of joy.

But nonetheless, you are a little dawn, a fantasy to reap, a
novelty of mind, an experience to feel and oversee—

As you see yourself.

Part II

Chapter 17

QUESTIONING OUR FOUNDATIONS

Learn from yesterday, live for today, hope for tomorrow. The important thing is not to stop questioning.
—Albert Einstein

Which of Our Basic Physical Assumptions Are Wrong—If Any?

Is there a beginning to the universe? *(issue 1)*
Is thermodynamics absolute? *(issue 2)*
Continuous motion by way of natural forces—yes, it is true. *(issue 3)*

I am writing this chapter to outline some concepts; later chapters will address more specifics. As many of these questions simply have no answers [1], this chapter does challenge some of our basic laws of physics if viewed narrowly. For example, if we understand that I am not violating the actual requirements of thermodynamic laws, but instead, working outside of their requirements, then my views on continuous motion become possible.

Our basic assumptions of facts about science and life are askew in many facets, as we are still neophytes when it comes to knowledge and its boundless or infinite reaches not yet discovered. Many of our scientific premises to date have merit and rest as pillars upon the shoulders of our elders, but they should not always be held sacrosanct, as there is much to unravel and much that never will be unraveled.

In other words, the finite mind is limited in scope. It is circumscribed by definition, and therefore can never know all things or infinite things. If an infinite sentient mind could know all things, it would create a circumscribed infinity. Infinity has no alpha nor omega, no space, no time, and yet all time and all space, all at one time.

Hence, infinity cannot be traditionally defined. If it could be, it would no longer be infinite; it would have parameters and become finite. Infinity is an anomaly to finite sentiency. *It always has been and always will be—period.* Mathematicians know this reality just as any supercomputer does as well; factoring infinity into a logical sense would burn up any supercomputer to resolve an infinite numbered question. *Note:* It is surprising that we as self-aware beings do not more regularly fry our own gray matter attempting to solve the reality of infinity, which is infinitely unsolvable. Infinity is the ultimate mystery; we are all trapped within infinity for all time. It is a claustrophobic nightmare to some people, I am sure. It is a certain truth forever undefined, save in undefined terms.

This predicament gives us limitless life seeking knowledge, as knowledge is infinite. That is the beauty of science and the truths it provides on a daily basis. Any other knowledge outside of science is of a meta basis and is suspect always to humankind's limitless invented knowledge, mythologies, and wishful thinking. Science is a venture to the contrary. It is the face of truth, even though the full truth is never fully known. If you want to believe in a truth, science is a nine-to-one bet versus meta-science, shaman or spiritual beliefs, and the mythologies that once acted as the basis for all knowledge. With the advent of science, we broke out of invented knowledge and found a home much closer to what is true. Still, the ironic part of this story is that meta-science is the cloaked truth we seek to unravel day by day.

The journey of science is the actual face of God, if one believes in such things. Science is certainly the closest thing to truth's journey we will ever engage in in our lifetimes.

Is there a beginning to the universe (outside of our big bang)?

No is the simple answer. However, some may ask what is meant by a beginning. Well, in a scientific realm, I believe you could argue that a beginning is born in every moment, and therefore, your answer might be a *yes* to the question above.

In other words, infinity has no beginning, no start point. However, it could be said that it therefore begins in every moment, since it cannot have an end or beginning. You see, something always has to have been somewhere at all times. It is an absurd notion to suggest that nothing ever existed. It is a double negative. It just is not real. Therefore, every moment within time and space is all there is or will ever be. There is no beginning and no end.

Now as far as our big-bubble universe known as the big bang, it had a beginning, about 13.8 billion years ago, but it exists in a much larger universe called infinity, so it is no bigger than a proton within a speck of sand. Actually, it is much smaller, beyond definition, because it is part of infinity. Crazy stuff? Perhaps. But that is the way the world turns, believe it or not!

This is the bizarre reality that provides us with life as finite creatures. It could not be any other way. We are forever trapped in a continuum that defies understanding, as again, to understand it would be to define it. And as I have said, anything defined is not infinite. So as a finite being, you are forever separated from the infinite, and vice versa. Yet the infinite and finite work together. Now explain that.

Issues two and three, *listed above at the start of this chapter,* are very much in conjunction with one another:

Is thermodynamics absolute? And *can continuous motion be true?*

Regarding thermodynamics: no. But in many ways, yes. Between quantum mechanics and relative mechanics, we have some nuanced differences that are being uncovered more and more. For example, refer to "The Long Arm of the Second Law" [2].

Additionally, the laws of thermodynamics are constricted within the parameters of relative heat and motion. They do not take into account the nature of the natural forces, such as magnetism, gravity, and static electromagnetism, in a realm that is harbored by both linear and nonlinear motions. As I will explain later, as such, continuous motion, not perpetual motion, becomes possible. I use the term *continuous*, rather than *perpetual*, because materials wear out, they atrophy and need replacement, so *continuous motion* is a more accurate term, albeit the net effect is essentially perpetual motion, which is only possible if you use the abundance of natural energies, not fossil fuels. Fossil fuels are bound by thermodynamic laws.

Continuous motion is possible via a couple of mechanical approaches. I first developed the idea of magnetics when I was a young preadolescent boy, but later moved on to using electrostatics along with gravity to achieve the same result. I will outline both the electrostatic method and secondarily the gravity and magnetic method for the purposes of this essay. However, my emphasis will be on the electromagnetic and gravity system working together with both linear and non-linear motion to leverage energy continuously.

This is scientific heresy because it appears to violate thermodynamic laws, but as I will repeat: the process does not use the materials required by thermodynamics; it uses natural and abundant energies, which are exempt from some thermodynamic requirements.

The concept is remarkably simple. please refer to chapter 30, "Our Universe, Science, and Potentials in Review.".

The essence of this chapter, again, is to follow up on some earlier documents I have written and important concepts that would change the world as we know it today. It would unify our species as we more fully use science to ameliorate our differences into a unified form.

I have been brief in this essay on purpose; I am usually much more verbose. If you find what I have to share of some interest, I hope it challenges your interests and you will pursue it to greater lengths. Only good can eventually come of it. That is my greatest hope.

[1] See "Big Questions in Life," chapter 28.
[2] J. Miguel Rubin, "The Long Arm of the Second Law," *Scientific American*, October 2008, pp. 63–67.

Chapter 18

Does Space Curve around Mass?

For the wise man looks into space and he knows there is no limited dimensions.
—Lao Tzu

I find this subject of great interest. Mass and inertia/gravity, coupled with time and space, are a tangled web duly woven. Their inscrutable truths give us our very breaths of life.

To my main points:

First, we need to dispel the notion of curved space. This is another concept derived from the concepts of the speed of light and mass/inertia intervening. Space curving is not the truth of our obscure and infinitely indescribable existence.

It seems to me that time and space are immutable, along with perhaps gravity/inertia. Contrary to current belief, they are as fixed as the cognitive notion of existence itself, or as immutable as the fixed solution to a geometric equation.

Time and space have been determined to be changeable based on velocity and density, by way of relativity being an absolute, and consequently marry up into the term *space-time*. This singular term has merit, since combined time and space are the common objects of physical dimension as we understand them. The notions that time changes and that space curves are relative ways for language only to express the effects of gravity on those elements of energy and/or mass. *Curved space* and *time running slow* are even poetically acceptable terms, but not physically accurate facts.

Light only curves, as would any other object of mass, when gravity impacts it. Without gravity, it would not so-called curve. *Note:* Photons have mass, because they are in motion. Hence, they are impacted by mass. (Show me a non-moving photon, and I will show you no photon at all.) To think of photons as massless is also a misnomer, due to their movement. To be less confusing about what physically takes place during the curving of light (not space) is to describe the impacts of gravity on any object as simply changing the object's direction due to the force of gravity from a mass. You may call this curved space, but it only convolutes a simple picture into an unnecessary description that obscures physics.

Likewise, the so-called empirical experiments that demonstrate time slowing down involve a misnomer. Time does not slow down, whether at the event horizon, or with an atomic clock running under different velocity from another stationary atomic clock. Simply the mechanics of the (macro/micro) particles that operate the measurement tools (clocks) are impacted by gravity/inertia via high velocities and thus slow down both the quantum and relative pieces of the mechanical matter that operate the measuring devices (clocks). Time is not slowed down. Matter is slowed down by physical forces. Matter is not time. Time truly has no mass, that is, it does not curve.

These seem to be fairly intuitive assumptions, without the need for mathematics, yet we have yet to fully pursue these physical realities. Along with conveniently calling the so-called discovery of a potential Higgs-boson as the completion of the standard model of particle physics? But where is the graviton? Note: the graviton is a missing elementary particle, that is assumed to support gravity.

We are a long way from sanctifying relativity, or even thermodynamics, as even thermodynamics only addresses atrophying energies, not natural and continuous energies, which are again conveniently ignored.

We are infinite gray matters far away from such a conclusion. That is the joy and celebration of science's mission. It is an endless positive for the world to improve itself through science as we unravel the truths of life itself.

Chapter 19

BEYOND THE HIGGS BOSON AND MORE

What is time, but the existence of time and space? And what is space, but the existence of space and time?

I am writing this brief chapter to whoever would not challenge convention or sleeps while he or she is conscious. The big bang, or multiple big bangs, is not the genesis of time or space. Time and space, along with perhaps gravity, are the cosmological constants, regardless of the advent of our paltry finite big bang relative to infinity.

Time and space equate to infinity—*period*. Nor, perhaps, will some mutant big bang ever change that fact. Nor will the possible and important Higgs-Boson discovery change a great deal. Ultimate-Reality rests on the ever-unknown picture of infinity. Albeit our inscrutable infinity is not our mathematical or functional reality, as we are finite. So contrary to infinity, our finite knowledge of science and its advancement is essential to better the world.

Note: If a tree falls and no one is there to see it, it still falls. And let me add an even more inscrutable *Note:* Time and space in our finite world are different from infinities, as with infinity, they exist and do not exist. That is the paradox of infinity, just as a tree is not really there to fall in infinity. Ponder that!

From my point of view, anyone who denies this is respectfully myopic and naive. These are respectful comments that I cannot expunge, because they are not convenient or conventional.

I even will say that respectfully, this may be difficult to get one's thoughts around, because it could have some mind-numbing impacts—such as that we are a part of something larger than us, and therefore as finite beings, we will never understand the infinite. To do so would define infinity, and that is an oxymoron. Infinity would—if defined—become finite. Just the facts . . . Again, I have written this redundant chapter to reinforce fundamentals that it is paramount to understand if we are to move forward and improve life for all, not just some. I hope this adds some clarity.

Chapter 20

Thermodynamics and Errant Assumptions

Begin challenging your own assumptions. Your assumptions are your windows on the world. Scrub them off every once in a while, or the light won't come in.
—Alan Alda

Thermodynamics is broadly predicated on the assumption that fuels atrophy. Change that assumption by eliminating fossil fuels and replacing them by using natural energies—such as gravity, electrostatics, and magnetism, coupled with dimensional leverage—that use both linear and non-linear motions, and you change the fundamental assumptions that thermodynamics is founded upon.

That is the key to develop continuous motion.

What has prevented this reality is an almost theological form of faithful and myopic alignment with traditional assumptions. Change those assumptions, and we grow. Accept these same traditional assumptions, and we do not.

By the way, thermodynamics is simply the science of energy and heat, based on its mathematics that seemingly binds us to its rules. Thermodynamics works when we use typical energy sources, but change those sources and the rules are modified.

All truths are basic, and this is a basic truth. Adopt it in our gray matter, and we change the world. Ignore it, and we continue to flounder and stop from moving knowledge forward.

I have written on this subject for the last couple of years, but my notions have not gained any traction, at least publicly or personally. I implore those of you who read this to review my thoughts on this subject again in the handful of essays I have written. *Note: Nearly all of the science chapters have some element of this issue, and some are especially dedicated to it.* Together, they make a case for reviewing our assumptions about thermodynamics. Please review the potentials in these essays and share them with others as well. For an example, I had a gentleman write to me who finally put it together once he viewed tidal power with continuous tons of millions of gallons of water continuously flowing; he then wrote that thermodynamics does not address that issue, to paraphrase him. This is the edge of hope I believe we will find, and the world will change. And for the better.

It matters.

Chapter 21

The Light of Science's Eyes

There are those who look at things the way they are, and ask why . . . I dream of things that never were, and ask why not?
—Robert Kennedy

Suppose dark matter does not move, far-fetched as it may be; therefore it may not have mass, unlike dark energy that does move and runs the ultimate show in the end, much as gravity runs the show at the moment. Note, movement also creates mass, not only a Higgs-boson. Just ask gravity, which only plays with motion/mass, or a photon, which creates mass through movement and hence bends due to gravity.

Essential interactions, excluding dark energy for the moment, are interactions of mass (movement and gravity). Those two elements portend our existence as particle physics suggests, but the monumental strides in the knowledge born from particle physics still has monumental strides yet to go to understand the fuller picture of how dark energy, dark matter, and neutrinos paint a more true understanding of life, mass, and matter, in other words, existence. For instance, mass is derived from movement, not solely or even potentially from the Higgs boson, as currently proposed.

We are neophytes in our plight to understand space, time, and gravity, along with their piece parts known as particle physics, which include yet the unknown, such as dark energy, dark matter, and the mysterious particles known as neutrinos, among other highly probable unknown particles.

We are simply on a journey—endlessly.

The mysteries of leptons, quarks, bosons, and their siblings, among other infinite mysteries such as time and space, and I would argue potentially gravity, combine into the trio of the infinite and offer an endless maze for the mind to explore, chase, and dream forevermore.

Our current assumptions may be very askew, and maybe not so, but the possibilities certainly energize my pea brain and those brains much more exotic than mine.

The task of our research is endless and exciting, but I would always caution not to hang your hat on a predecessor's conceptions, such as thermodynamics has done. There is more to the picture than such assumptive absolutes.

We are only beginning. And the landscape never ends as we paint our ultimate logic, along with assumptive possibilities, that will together open doors not yet unlocked. In other words, our logic today is not sacrosanct; at best it is open-ended, and to consider our current logic absolute is to blind one eye. We need both mind's eyes open to keep the lights on forever and a day!

Cheers in the exciting and endless journey of science and philosophy.

Chapter 22

LIFE'S JOURNEY

In school, I could hear the leaves rustle and go on a journey.
—Clint Eastwood

This journey of life is poised to hurt, harm, uplift, and surprise with joy. It is not structurally fixed based on good or bad, as everyone has his or her own varied paths and fortunes or lack thereof to manifest within. It is a fickle life, for which many people and life in general are cut short, but some are granted longevity; some live with silver spoons, and some with long-suffering—without rhyme or reason.

And that is the truth.

Even if you are of a deity-centric spirituality, it is no respecter in this argument. Note: Even the Christian New Testament is replete with statements from Peter and James that "God is no respecter of persons."

So why do so many suffer and are compelled to make the hardest of choices in life—to live or die—and others are granted the ease of a pleasant wind and soft floating driftwood, without a hardship to confront beyond the superficial?

It is not possible to know. All we can know is that no one is running this random show, for which so many win and so many lose, not by merit, but primarily by randomness of arbitration.

Some do work hard to win or to lose, but such hard work does not guarantee the result. The truth of life is a puzzle coined in purity, not in merit, save for a fleeting group, and even then, circumstances of a moment could uproot the hard work of those who have tried to do either wrong or right.

Life is the way it is.

For me, it makes no sense in the end except to try to do your best. The end is all we really come to, and all we can hope is that our legacy has some carryover for good. At least for me, that is my only truth.

My time is running out on the hourglass, and when the final curtain call is done, I can only hope it is a painless drifting off and fading into the abyss, which we all are a part of in the end.

I often think the greatest measure of success would be to be a natural optimist, free of fear.

That would be great, would it not? So here is hoping you find your optimism and freedom from fear in this fickle world we all are a part of!

If you are fortunate enough to find such a life, please take note of your grace, and give the goodness you have been blessed to have found—to the path of others.

Ponder your beginnings and endings—they are all you really have and by the manner for which you use them.

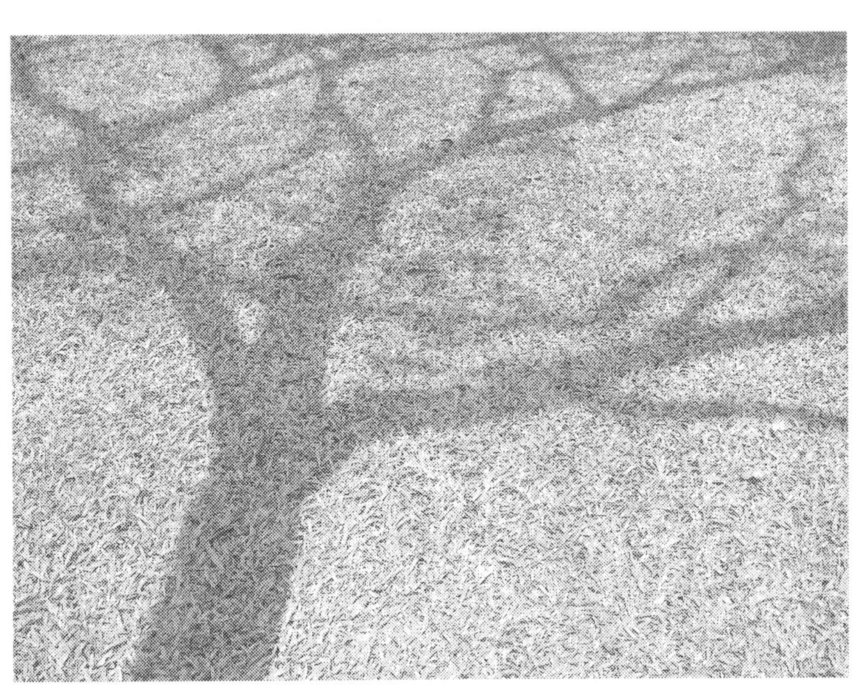

Chapter 23

COMMUNICATION PAST THE SPEED OF LIGHT—TRUE?

Nothing in the universe can travel at the speed of light, they say, forgetful of the shadow's speed.
—Howard Nemerov

When a photon is split and its companion responds thousands of kilometers away, at the same moment, we have communication that clearly bypasses the speed of light. We even know this can be done at a molecular level as well, thus boosting the potential impact or movement.

Movement is the equivalent of mass, and mass can be converted into energy. Hence we have the rudiments for power coupled with the ultimate for communication speed, which is not hinged on the speed of light, but on the firm mysteries of quantum mechanics.

Further, when it is recognized that a companion proton or molecule has changed, this has the fundamental potential to communicate intelligently, if you had millions of receptors to interpret an ASCII (128 seven-bit combination) character. This proposition, of course, is monumental, perhaps even an unrealistic task to design, but it conceptually is possible. Thus, information theoretically can supersede the speed of light, again in spite of those who would argue that you cannot transfer information beyond the speed of light. But *note:* At the simplest level, once you see a companion particle or molecule change direction, spin, or electric output, you know the other distant companion has signaled a change for you or itself. This is simple confirmation of information trumping the speed of light. It lacks sophistication, but it is a single solitary hail for which no speed of light can compete.

With more time and scientific development, who knows what is possible? That is a fact. To assume and sit on the laurels of thermodynamics or other potentially limited concepts is to live in the past, much like we once did with mythology and superstitions from invented human knowledge.

The precursor of knowledge is change, growth, and expansion of the past to infinity.

Chapter 24

BIG-BANG PARADIGM SHIFT

A long habit of not thinking a thing wrong gives it a superficial appearance of being right.
—Thomas Paine

Pancake Universe
(Food for Thought)

Why does our universe appear to be flat? Well, it may follow the same principles as pancake batter, when gravity thrusts it onto a force field of matter called a skillet. It becomes flat and expansive instantaneously. Hence, possibly our so-called big-bang universe may not be the result of a heretofore singularity and wishful notion of inflation, but may be the result of a completely different paradigm.

I would note that the graviton has not been found as of yet, and may never be found, as gravity may be as ubiquitous and infinite as space is spaceless and time is timeless. Gravity may be an infinite player too. It may be that we live within the symphony of a trio, by adding gravity to our infinite duo of time and space.

Gravity is a curious fellow, as it is as weak as weak can be, and yet it is a force that is stronger than the speed of light at the event horizon or within black holes. This variable source of energy may be our missing link to the theory of a big bang. However, perhaps it was a splatter on a field such as a brane rather than a big bang—that gave us our inflationary splatter.

The forces of the universe(s) and its hidden realities, known for now as dark matter and dark energy, may be more than mere space fillers; they may be our branes: they may be a yet unknown that has the force of a skillet pan combined with the force of gravity's greatest strengths that made our physically flat universe. Two branes colliding may cause a splatter, known today as the big bang.

It is a story worth pursuing, as our geometric physics holds this as a possibly logical truth.

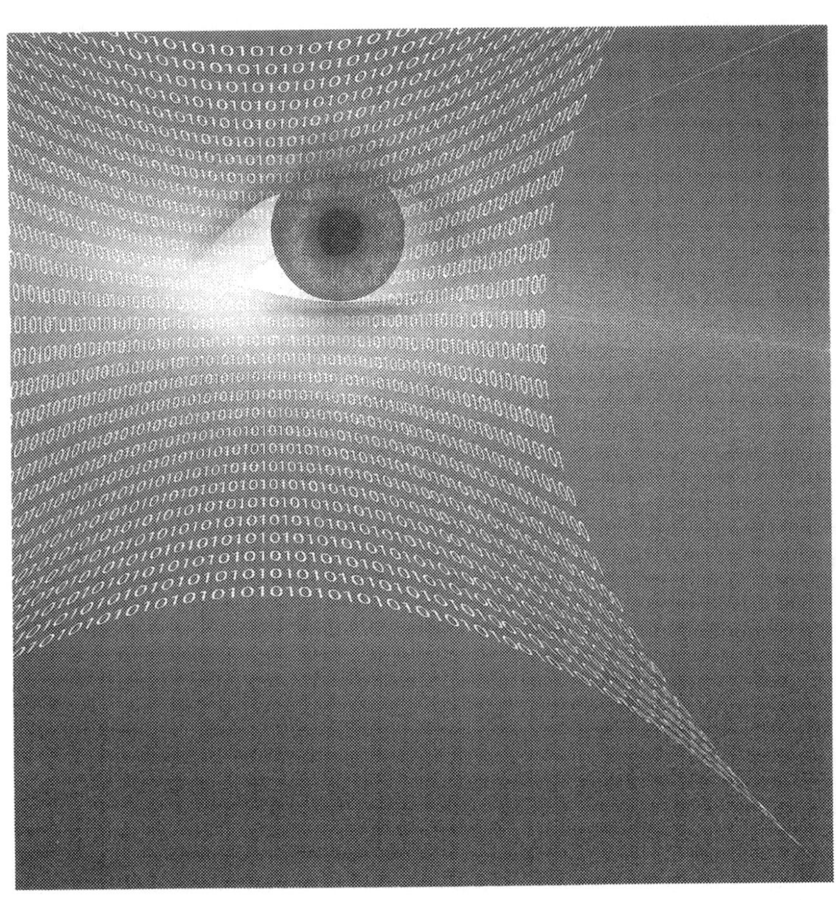

Chapter 25

Physics Issues That Raise Eyebrows

Paradoxical and precise at the same time—that is physics.

There is a broad and engaging article on existentialism in *New Scientist* magazine (July 23–29, 2011). It is a well-put-together series of articles. However, I would like to make a few points that seem to elude conversation, almost as if we have assumed what we really cannot know to be true except by intuition.

I want to identify in the next few items below some physics issues that could use some further review and commitment, too, as we look for the Holy Grail of physics—knowledge that will propel us into a future whereby we are enabled to treat each other much better. These issues are often bypassed, but are important to move closer to the truth of existence.

Number 1 Issue: Paraphrasing a comment by Alan Guth [1], "Perhaps something is nothing." This statement is brilliant. It is that the balance of the cosmos will continue to stand the test of time, but never find its final proof, as infinity will always curtail that reality. *Please additionally read chapter 32, "Everything Is Nothing, and Nothing Is Everything," as in truth, the big-bang universe is no more than a mere speck in the scheme of space and time, even smaller than a neutrino's smallest known size. Just as entanglement and superposition trump all space and time, the classical physics it hails from as an ultimate truth is theory only.*

Number 2 Issue: Note: Most writers and thinkers involved with physics or philosophy tend to assume that time and space were somehow nonexistent before the big bang. That seems a novel or naive perspective, as no one really knows, especially when coupled with an implicit fact, that infinity by definition has *no beginning and no end.* In other words, something is always there, here, and everywhere all the time!

I personally sense that time and space have been the whipping boys and girls of assumptive physics for far too long, such as assuming that space and time curve, and so on. Only relative to mass do space or its particles move or so-called curve, as anything so-called curves always relative to gravity. *Note:* From this assumption, we have created all forms of novel thinking, such as time travel back to the past. Good luck on that assumption from a sentient perspective.

Number 3 Issue: Inflation is assumed to have happened because it fits our needs to understand the CMB (cosmic microwave background) and so on. But just as Alan Guth poignantly pointed out, *"Perhaps something is nothing."* So perhaps entanglement, which violates time and space and the speed of light, was the beginning trigger, not simply a so-called singularity. It is a thought worth examination.

Number 4 Issue: Gravity is always called the weakest force relative to its counterparts, only I would add, gravity is relative, or in other words, always variable dependent upon its environment. For instance: gravity trumps all forces at the realm of a black hole, but acts like near massless quarks, next to one another in a micro-environment, and is no doubt impacted by other dark energy and dark matter, along with its other three forces at a quantum level. Therefore, gravity at the quantum level is weak, but not nonexistent. *So the four forces we know of are unified*, as they are relative to the environment they reside in, and therefore electrons do not eventually collapse into the nuclei, but they do grapple with gravity.

However, I do not believe that classical physics and quantum physics are unified, only the four forces. Again, review my own personal essay on this subject, chapter 32, "Everything Is Nothing, and Nothing Is Everything." The thoughts I express in that chapter is why Alan Guth, a cosmologist from MIT, really caught my eye, as noted above.

Number 5 Issue: Smart energy now is the greatest potential for the human race to build unity that I can currently envision. Please look for section 3 called "Smart Energy Now" in chapter 30, "Our Universe, Science, and Potentials in Review." This section in brief explores the development of continuous motion, not perpetual motion as all things atrophy, using our natural forces: electrostatics, gravity, and magnetism, versus the need for fossil fuels. It is in this area that I have several working models in mind, and would like to work with a physicist, with the mathematical language of science, to optimize its development. This is implicitly doable, but most physicists will invoke the second law of thermodynamics to derail the effort. Make no mistake: this is an area the world is headed toward, as even the second law is not sacrosanct and uses variables that are myopic. See J. Miguel Rubin's article "The Long Arm of the Second Law" [2] for some further thoughts about this issue. Additionally, thermodynamics, again, is based on a set of principles that involve classic reaction-for-action mechanics. I bypass some of thermodynamics by using natural forces, such as tidal forces, that are continuous.

[1] Comment by Alan Guth, Cosmo 2011logist @ MIT, Magazine Article: "*Why Is There Something Rather Than Nothing?*" July 23–29, 2011 *New Scientist*, p. 28.

[2] J. Miguel Rubin, "The Long Arm of the Second Law," *Scientific American*, October 2008, 63–67.

Chapter 26

Continuous Motion, Not Perpetual Motion

A perpetual holiday is a good working definition of hell.
—George Bernard Shaw

Continuous motion and perpetual motion are two actually unrelated subjects, but they both possess a perpetual quotient as you define them. They also are on the fringes of physics, and they do not receive the due respect they actually merit, as they open the possibilities to changing life as we know it for the better. Why? you might ask. Well, they build on knowledge, which is always a good thing, but more important, the import of perpetual motion can change the world and bring us closer as a community of peoples. Such knowledge and its power take diversity and unify it, lessening warring behaviors and improving communication.

If you read my "Smart Energy Now" in section 3 of chapter 30, "Our Universe, Science, and Potentials in Review," you will have a better understanding of what I am trying to explain here. This is just a starting point to generate the mind's interest in matters that can pay in humanity's most valued dividends *perpetually*.

A. Perpetual (Continuous) Motion

Perpetual (continuous) motion is a product, not of the second law of thermodynamics, but the mechanics of simple motion, multiplied by both linear and non-linear directions, propelled by natural forces, that is, gravity, electrostatics, and magnetism or a varied combination of those three natural forces coupled with different linear and angular motions.

When these principles of motion and natural energies work together, they establish continuous motion. I use the term *continuous* rather than *perpetual* because materials (matter) wear out and need replacement at some point. But for all intents and purposes, you could sensibly call this perpetual motion.

All it requires is an understanding of motion in all its forms and nature's self-propelled energies, as I mentioned earlier. Hence, thermodynamics is not an applicable theology or science with these conditions because you are not putting into something less than you are receiving. You are merely leveraging a form of gear ratio via nature's natural elements and dimensions, whereby you gain more than you use, because we are not involved with loss for gain, such as in burning a fuel for energy. This process is therefore exempt from thermodynamics.

B. Motion Equals Mass

Motion is mass. Since all things are in motion, the idea of a massless particle is flawed exponentially.

Yet we keep asserting such particles, such as photons and gravitons, are massless. Show me a photon without motion, and I will show you a world without form or electromagnetism as we know it. It does not exist.

Now, I will surmise that dark matter may be of a motionless nature, which defies identification or form in a traditional sense. Such a motionless mathematical formula tied to our motion-based world may be the balance and genesis that makes sense and will lead to new vistas of knowledge, along with a new vista of questions.

Time will tell.

Still, my presumption for dark matter is just that: a random leap into the possibilities, without a scrap of knowledge, only presumptions for the speculative mind to ponder. More central to my theme is that motion produces mass, and we are captives to that mass-based world in all we do or know today.

Show me a massless particle, and I will show you a measurement system that is lacking.

Further on this subject: Does that enigmatic world of a black hole exude the impression of density so great as to imply no motion or the restriction thereof? However, it would then take the opposite to achieve a black hole, which has a motion quotient that is faster than the speed of light, to reflect its own existence. Hence, once again, motion equals mass on a weighted particle scale relative to its motion.

So the question arises: at an ultimate density, if that were possible, does motion cease? And if it ceases, what transpires at that moment? A big bang, a new dimension, or even dark matter or even dark energy?

These are the questions I find of intriguing interest. Foremost, however, is continuous motion, based upon non-thermodynamic mathematics as the forces used are not subject to thermodynamic rules; thus, our theories of heat diminution must take on a new math, based on natural energy and converging motions. For a clear example, simply review tidal ocean forces, which are endless, at least in relative terms of everyday life. Continuous motion clearly exists, but without thorough review or practical exploitation. *Again, see chapter 30, section 3, for a more thorough explanation of "Smart Energy Now."*

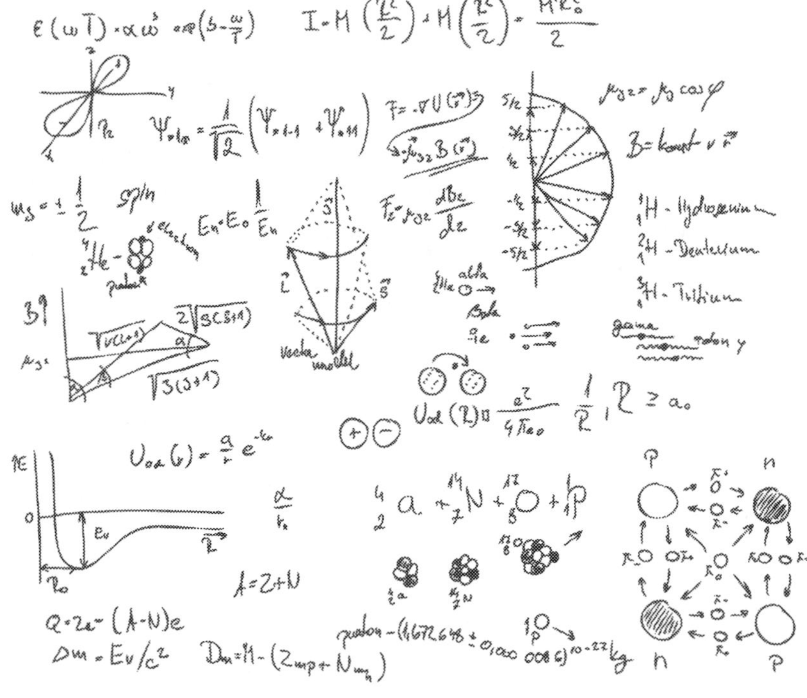

spin
A=Z+N
p
n

Chapter 27

The Prism of Physics: Hopes, Goals, and Realities

To dream the impossible dream.
—Joe Darion, *Man of La Mancha*

Thermodynamics is threaded through the firm notions of relativity's mathematics. In other words, force, mass, and movement or acceleration are seemingly straightforward when mathematics is defined and applied against the backdrop of the rules defined by thermodynamics.

By the way: thermodynamics is simply the science of energy and heat, based on mathematics that seemingly bind us to its rules.

With exception, if the force, mass, and acceleration are manipulated in combination by both linear and non-linear directions of thermodynamic movement, based on using the forces of simple gravity, among other natural energy sources, then the results will differ from the traditional fixed notions of our heretofore science of thermodynamics. But as of yet, no one seems to understand this or has manifested such an application.

Entropy and the other rules of thermodynamics, while inevitable, just as a *common shoe* with use, will become worn out with time; you also can extend that worn-out shoe a hundredfold, rather than like for like or reaction for action equivalency. In other words, energy is only lost based on an equal level of energy applied. However, energy can be applied with a ratio basis that mathematically creates more reaction for an action than a like-for-like result. Thus, you can create a virtually continuous-motion machine, with the exception of parts eventually wearing out and needing to be replaced.

If my hypothesis is true, then we change the very dimensions of the world in almost every discipline that you can imagine. And all for the better.

I would hope someone with a physics or electromechanical background would contact me. And please read some of my science-specific chapters, especially chapter 26, "Continuous Motion, Not Perpetual Motion," as I hope they will shed some further light on this subject.

This type of purely physics-based/mathematical-energy solution will additionally bring us together as a single human race of people, rather than as disparate groups competing harmfully with each other. This physics can change the world in personal matters as well as mathematical ones.

Note: We live within confined thinking built upon the philosophical and mechanical rules of the past. For instance, does the concept of inflation at the start of the big bang hold to Einstein's cosmic speed limit of light? No. But we make adjustments in our thinking to accommodate that seeming violation of physics. Similarly, thermodynamics has some areas that bend as well. But they bend within the confines of logical mathematics, which we have simply not explored as of yet. I would also note that the brane contention for the infinite quest of explaining history and time is a true possibility.

The open fields of physics and mathematics are unbounded infinities, which are in bloom at every moment for the taking by those who seek truth. However, the real truth is that many a truth was discovered by mistake! But—oh well, I digress.

Clearly truth is holding at bay our preformed modes of thoughts. Docked in self-made impressions, or in other words, our scotomas (blind spots), just waiting to sail away and change the symphony of infinity's seas, which reality holds forever open.

The possibilities of physics, of mathematics, of the progression of reason, hold the hope of the ages, the Holy Grail of truth, not from the static fixations of the past, but from the knowledge born in the moment, from the shoulders of the past and our ever-evolving future, born of our moments to moments.

Chapter 28

BIG QUESTIONS IN LIFE

Philosophy begins in wonder.
—Plato

We do not have the answers to the big questions in life *(infinity, the beginning, the end of time, God, and so on)* and never will.

To be clear, I am an agnostic, as I find I must be to be honest with myself. I neither believe nor disbelieve in a so-called God or gods. I simply cannot know, nor does it matter in the bigger picture of ethics and doing right by others.

And by the way, our universe (from the big bang) is a mere drop in the bucket; in fact, it's the actual size of a proton in the bigger scheme of space. That is what is so fundamentally fickle when we try to answer questions such as these; and if there is a God, how did that evolve? In point of fact, for me, infinity is timeless and spaceless, as it always has been, which defies our sense of logic.

But when you think about it, if it were not there before, something had to be in its place. So knowledge of such things is, as I have said, purely a concept based only on faith, not fact. And that is a fact. Archaeologists believe that early humankind, about 35,000 years ago, began to bond through shamans and their spiritual-type rituals. They found a community in such beliefs. Then came a few cultures that believed in similar virgin births, until our final one about two thousand years ago with the birth of Jesus. And after about four hundred years after his death, the formation of the Catholic Church deified him by a vote of Catholic monks; it was a contentious vote to gain better control over society. Or so that is how I see it. Many Christian sects did not believe in his deity. The Gnostics, for one, who simply believed that living a good life, as Jesus did, built the only true foundation for goodness and so-called being saved or redeemed in the eyes of any possible deity.

This is the model of Jesus that I follow as a role model, along with Albert Schweitzer, Gandhi, and Dr. Martin Luther King. These are individuals committed to high standards and goodness, rather than an eye for an eye.

I would note that even Mohammed, who was the founder of Islam, believed in and followed Jesus. Few people really know this fact. But then came science with new truths that violated the written invented truths of mankind, such as only being here for about five or six thousand years on earth and God created man and all things. The Judeo-Christian Bible's absolute truths had to give way to science as concubines, slaves, and killing infidels were abhorrent to modern man's sense of humanity; but of course, the other human-made rhetoric of the Bible, such as homosexual conduct and so on, remains selectively sacrosanct in sections of Leviticus and Deuteronomy. The early Bible set the stage for what became a horrible holocaust that early religious wars, the burning of thousands of witches, and similar tragedies were fought over. Competing texts allowed for killing infidels.

Well, science has prevailed in most of the modern world today. But past ravages from, again, selective biblical and Quran-based rhetoric are still practiced today, and even seem to be returning to new stature.

I will repeat my consistent theme throughout my chapters: the Golden Rule and doing no harm should be in practice through the United Nations as a common and absolute standard. Therefore, any culture, religion, or belief system that violates these fundamental laws of *doing no harm* and living by the *Golden Rule* needs to be altered or abolished. This should be the prime charter of the United Nations.

Just think about it: God or Allah wants infidels killed, but also believes in universal love? The hypocrisy and lack of intellect is stunning, to say the least, in the vast gray matter of the human race.

I believe Mark Twain said it best: *"If there were another race besides the human race, I would join it."*

My point of this chapter is simple: live for goodness, not cruelty, and you will follow your God or goodness in the truest of manners.

And that is what actually matters—*end of story.* Any other proposition is of evil and will simply cause humanity to needlessly suffer.

What is your choice?

Chapter 29

THE FINITE AND THE INFINITE

I am incapable of conceiving infinity, and yet I do not accept finity.
—Simone de Beauvoir

Finite and infinite: the Holy Grail that will never meet, humanity's paradox. Well, it is about the twain of our finite and infinite worlds we are bound within. And a twain that will never meet but in that disparate truth; we simply are bound to grow for the better, as we are more similar than otherwise.

So goes our hope for knowing all things, for our capability to understand in total what science or faith pursues, not in vain, but certainly in failure, comprehensively speaking.

Mathematics is the very face of god, if you will, or in other terms: the face of truth and the goal to understand what the mind is capable of understanding. Beyond that finite reality is an infinite reality where even math breaks down and fails; for infinity is real, and no mathematics is capable of defining infinity. Just ask a math major. (Math majors can identify it, but they will never define it.)

So it is true for us of sentient minds, which reach for our understanding of infinity, for purpose, or for that notion of ultimate truth, or search for a god from within our finite existences. Again, our comprehensive understanding of all nature will fail, and it will always be so, as long as we are finite beings within an infinite realm.

This is the dilemma for those who believe in a scientific understanding of existence of the universe, the real universe, not just our big-bang universe, which is no more than the size of a single proton in the true scheme of spatial reality or, in other words, within our infinite reality.

We are captives of nature beyond our understanding as long as we remain finite beings. Only an infinite structure, which by definition cannot be circumscribed by definition, can in theory know the truth of all things. In fact, it can be argued that as an infinite structure or being, there is no such thing as knowing or knowledge, ego, and the like. Infinity is without awareness, as awareness itself would be a defined circumscribing and therefore limiting element that would preclude infinity. This is a conundrum of the first degree, but that is what infinity is—indefinable, *period*.

Factually, to believe in your capability to have any simple or complex perception of infinity is to manifest a limited definition of infinity, and therefore you violate the principle of infinity, which cannot be defined.

Hence, we grapple with the ultimate conundrum of our very existence, of our finite and infinite worlds, which will never meet by way of knowledge.

Mathematics teaches us this truth, and sentient wisdom would do well to accept this truth.

Simply we live in an infinite fog, but by way of a finite existence. So find your truth inside the scope of your own space and time of life. And make it a good truth, one based on the Golden Rule and pursue knowledge at every crossroad of life.

That is all we have—nothing more, nothing less.

Cultures, religions, and fads can be good or bad, but they are all vain and vacuous unless they operate by truth and the Golden Rule.

That is where we exist, accept it or not.

Again, infinities are our reality, which precludes our ultimate fullness of knowledge, but also gives us an endless pursuit to grow—hopefully for the better! This truth makes us more similar than disparate, and this truth will enable growth to embrace a reality that improves on our lives and those of the people about us.

P.S. This is a refrain of chapter 15, "It Only Takes One Thing" (the Golden Rule), with a coupling of my chapters on science and the value science manifests for us all.

Chapter 30

OUR UNIVERSE, SCIENCE, AND POTENTIALS IN REVIEW

Quantum physics thus reveals a basic oneness of the universe.
—Erwin Schrodinger

For what it's worth, please ponder and enjoy!

Section 1

The Quantum—from which we all arise . . .

Even though quantum gravity currently seems to be a missing link, the quantum is gravity's birthplace, as suspected by little old me, from which all matter and energy originate. I postulate, however, that time and space are exempt from an inscrutable beginning, as they are infinite, just as possibly is gravity and other natural forces are, but that is a question we may never have an absolute answer to. If we ever find the graviton particle, it would help the discussion, but that is also a missing link.

The origins of all finite creation come from the quantum, at least this is the most we can hope to ever understand, as all else is of an infinite realm, and the infinite is not and will never be definable in terms that finite sentient beings can understand.

Our universe(s) conscious understanding, or rather foundation, is built upon the solitary empire of quantum building blocks.

That is principle 1. The quantum is our foundation in all we will come to understand—and perhaps, we may even glimpse at its predecessor's trigger. Therefore, always define your mathematics and philosophical notions of space and time in conjunction with all of the natural forces we are ruled by, based on their quantum roots. The current notion of space-time is highly likely askew. I would suggest that all things are quantized. Remember: even a straight line or circles are arguably a combination of bits.

So whether gravity, as well as space and time, is quantized at a subatomic micro-level and/or a macro-level, or perhaps morph in the process or not, please remember that natural forces are created equal at a base level, even as space and time are constants within both infinity and a finite existence.

However, in the examination of nature and the truth of our existence of matter and energy, the question often becomes, what is the beginning or the end? I would offer that such a question can never be answered, as the alpha and the omega are of an infinite nature, which will never be defined by finite mathematics or philosophy. To define *infinity* would be to no longer make it infinite. In other words, you cannot circumscribe infinity; if you could define infinity, it would logically no longer be infinite, but finite.

Infinity by definition and nature is not definable.

This is principle 2: the infinite is not and never will be defined by the finite, or differently said, by finite sentiency.

And finally, principle 3 (which I would assume will create the most controversy among modern-day physicists and perhaps some philosophers) is that space and time are immutable (fixed and unchangeable). They do not change, even at the event horizon, nor does time curve. Anything physical, does curve relative to gravity's influence. *Note:* I will argue in the next section, "*Science Is Infinitely More Than It Seems,*" that contrary to previously miscalculated scientific testing, from my biased point of view, time and space do not change via acceleration or lack thereof. Time and space, as all things, are impacted by gravity, but not to the point of changing space or time. I will soon explain.

Additionally, as you read this book, perhaps rather than beginning with the principles of thermodynamics as sacrosanct, I would suggest you try to begin with these principles, which I have outlined above, and our math and science will thereby define our physical empire and its riches, since virtually infinite energy will be manifest, for all practical descriptions' purposes, from the simple and logical mechanics these three principles portend.

These riches, which I speak of, I believe will help unite the world in common union for the good.

Section 2

Science Is Infinitely More Than It Seems (Classic, Relativity (Macro-World), and Quantum (Micro-World)

Classic and Quantum physics underpin one another, but they are not based on the same math or logic. They are distinct in dimension is the best way I would describe them.

Theoretical physics is hard enough to follow, let alone understand, as it has its own language and bizarre concepts that actually defy the logic of the world we live within. For instance, the concept of entanglement, whereby micro-sized particles millions of miles apart respond to one another or communicate as if they were local to each other, whereby the speed of light does not apply, is a proven phenomenon, also known as locality and non-locality behavior. The jargon of classical mathematics and quantum mechanics or the macro and micro worlds do not operate the same. This is confusing, much as the concept of *infinity*—that which has no beginning and no end—is an impossible term to grasp. But I am printing my thoughts here for the few of you who may be involved with quantum physics and may be able to possibly forward my thoughts on to a forum that may take up the issues I raise below. It is my shot in the dark to convey issues that have since my early adolescence and even younger captured my imagination. I do hope some of you find it of interest.

So read at your own will. As I have stated, the language and concepts do really require some background in this bizarre field of quantum mechanics to really even get close to grasping what is being explained. I also take my own liberties with my own conceptions to further confuse the issues. However, my goal is to clear up what I believe to be some former misconceptions. Clearly, to many of you, much of this will seem a grand heresy, but I would ask that you consider the broad scope of what we still do not know; we still may be errant in our current understandings regarding physics' so-called proven laws.

The search for the unified theory of nature or existence is a fickle road in conventional terms quite simply because we live within an existence that is inscrutably possessed of infinity. Infinities cannot and will not succumb to classic mathematics. In fact, classical mathematics breaks down and is void outside of the macro-world (relativity) or the real world of objects that we live within.

We also live within the micro-world or particle-world of quantum mechanics, which are the building blocks of our object world, made from atoms, quarks, electrons, photons, and so on, along with the world of what is known as entanglement and superpositions, which defy all classical or common logic. Quite clearly, just as infinity defies explanation, if you try to extrapolate or describe entanglement and superpositions in mathematical terms, it simply will not and cannot be done.

That is why I would call the quantum world, which underpins and creates our "real world," the fifth dimension. In other words, there are the three physical dimensions (up/down, back/forward, and side to side), plus time, plus the quantum or infinity realms, which are separate dimensions in my view. And both the macro—and micro-worlds contain the four forces we know of in the physics world as the strong, weak, electromagnetic, and gravity forces. These forces are the glue and engine of the dimensions we exist within. I understand the argument about the search for the fleeting notion of quantum gravity, but as I stated it earlier in this chapter, quantum mechanics is the bearer or source of all physical things, and gravity is one of them. If you have mass, you have gravity. If you have no mass, you are subject to gravity's influence. *Note:* With the exception of entanglement, which is a mystery that I believe has its roots in non-particle, wave science. But that is perhaps a question that will defy explanation, much as infinity forever will.

I would also add two sub-dimensions to the quantum world: particle and wave. These are the transmission modes of the micro—and macro-worlds. They do behave quite differently, and often in tandem, unlike they always do in the macro-world or object-world we live our daily lives within.

- Quantum particle transport is based on the speed of light, as defined by Albert Einstein.
- Wave transport, I would argue, is a continuous (connected) method of transport that allows for entanglement to occur. In my opinion, quantum entanglement represents the concept of infinity in action; it is a non-locality-based transport that is always connected, as if all separated objects were based on the concept of locality. Waves are connected, making the notion of everything, nothing and nothing, everything all at the same moment in time. This is where classical math breaks down and we have to rely on a new methodology and understanding of time and space; hence, infinity to describe existence per se. It is that complicated and that simple—or indescribable.

For accuracy's sake, there may be five or six more dimensions if string theory is correct, but those are of the quantum micro-world, bound to the indefinable quantum dimension we are infinitely bound to.

I am a layperson with a basic understanding of the world in which we live. These realms or dimensions are the basics; we are both simplistically born into and currently they are all we are capable of understanding. But *understanding* is a qualified term, as some things can and cannot be understood—the paradox of existence.

With the passing of time, which is a misnomer in its own right given the special theory of relativity, which I will explain in a moment, we will expand our understanding, and thus increase our knowledge of the forever and infinitely non-understandable. That is the ultimate truth we are compelled to as finite beings existing within an infinite realm. Simply, we are always and infinitely expanding our knowledge. In other words, some things are not understandable, given that you are a finite being within an infinite realm. *Finite* by definition cannot grasp the infinite. This is both a philosophical point as well as a mathematical, as they are synonymous, due to the fact that classical mathematics, as I have stated before, breaks down at the point of some aspects of the quantum world and its entanglement or infinite underpinnings that allow our world, or our very existence, to occur.

I will use time, as we have defined it in classical mathematical terms, to illustrate, at least to me, that our perceptions of time today through the lens of Einstein's special relativity are not accurate.

As I explain my thought processes, keep in mind what I have said about the quantum (micro) and the relative (macro) worlds" or realms of physics: they are different in virtually every way. The macro—and micro-worlds are affected differently by gravity, by the tandem travel of *waves* and *particles* in the micro-world, and by entanglement among other inscrutable behaviors, foremost within quantum mechanics. They are of two dimensions, if you will.

Think of the very famous thought experiment of Schrodinger's cat. It is an illustrative, but bogus argument, in some respects, because it involves both the macro-world of the cat and the micro-world of quantum mechanics in order to enable the description of the cat being both alive and dead at the same time, or in a superposition. This can never be, as superpositions and entanglements are restricted to the quantum or micro-world of atomic particles. This is what has been done with speaking about an astronaut traveling at near the speed of light and behaving the same way as muons, or other elementary particles, such as electrons do. It is a spurious scenario that continues to mislead us as we explore time and space. Simply put, macro biology or physiology does not change with velocity, outside the normal changes that gravity imposes on impacting our normal heart or breathing rates. Yet we have continued to discount or ignore this monumental difference when we engage our mathematical or particle experiments. It is comparing apples to elephants!

The notion of time as changing due to the speed of travel is a misguided concept. It is accurate in theory, but not in fact. My theorem is "Time is immutable, just as space is. Both are underpinned by infinity and quantum mechanics, which dismantle classic mathematics and physics as we might hope to simply define them." This is a simple theorem that speaks clearly for itself.

In other words, time and space are fixed and outside of our finite understanding. They do not change, as special relativity implies, by curving or slowing down or speeding up dependent on speed and mass. They can be described as such in a quasi-manner, but in fact they remain as they are—infinite and inexplicable.

The current understanding of time is based on mass and velocity, or Einstein's special theory of relativity, but time is again, as I said, immutable and not subject to the speed of an object relative to its mass, but to its mass alone, subject to gravity. In other words, all objects will not slow down or speed up based on the speed by which we travel. The current experiments that use atomic clocks—one clock stationary and the other traveling at high speed, which then are used to measure their times, which are logically different—is fatally flawed. Time is affected by way of the mechanical operation of atomic clocks, which is influenced by the gravity or mass it experiences within its travel. Again in other words, if a clock is traveling at a high velocity, it experiences greater gravity in a shorter period of time, which alters its mechanical functions. Time does not actually change; only the forces of gravity that impact its mechanics change and slow down the clock's mechanical operation. Thus, density or gravity slows down or speeds up a clock's mechanical parts and physical time actuations. Time is not changed; only the operation of the clock subject to different mechanical pressures is changed. In simple terms, a clock's time is always going to be different based on its atmospheric conditions, that is, whether it is stationary on the ground at sea level or sitting on the highest mountain. The mechanics will work differently, but time itself has not changed; only the clock's mechanics have been altered by different pressures, so the times will be infinitesimally different. Extrapolate this using the speed of light and gravity's changes, and the clocks show much different time results. But again, time itself has not changed; only the physical apparatus that measures time has changed. Time, remember, is immutable—*period.*

Time has been manipulated by mixing the dimensions of classic mathematics' and quantum mechanics' realms as if they were one. They are not. This has distorted our perceptions of the immutable and unchangeable nature of time and the notions of a curved space. (Classic standard relativity and quantum mechanics are unique and distinct. It's that simple, and this premise of confusing the two with the same assumed mathematics has misled us, very understandably, but also very obviously.)

I will attempt to give an example.

We need to first dispel the notion of curved space. This is another concept derived from the concepts of the speed of light and mass. This is not the truth of our obscure and infinitely indescribable existence.

It seems to me that time and space are immutable. Contrary to current belief, they are as fixed as the cognitive notion of existence itself or as immutable as the fixed solution to a geometric equation.

Time and space have been determined to be changeable based on velocity and density, and consequently marry up into the term *space-time*. The singular term has merit, since combined time and space are the common objects of physical dimensions as we understand them. But the notion that time changes and that space curves are relative ways only for language to express the effects of gravity on these elements of energy and/or mass. *Curved space* and *time running slow* are even poetically acceptable terms, but not physically accurate facts.

Light only curves as would any other object of mass—when gravity impacts it. Without gravity, it would not so-called curve. To be less confusing about what physically takes place during the curving of light is to describe the impacts of gravity on any object as simply changing the object's direction due to the force of gravity. You may want to call this *curved space*, but it only convolutes a simple picture into an unnecessary description that obscures classical physics.

Likewise, the experiments that demonstrate time slowing down are a misguided misnomer. Time does not slow down, whether at the event horizon or with an atomic clock running under different velocity from another atomic clock. Simply, the mechanics of the (macro/micro) particles that operate the measurement tools (clocks) are impacted by gravity via high velocities and thus slow down both the quantum and standard relative pieces of mechanical matter that operate measuring devices. Time is not slowed down. Matter is the only element slowed down, by physical forces. Matter is not time. Time has no mass, that is, it does not curve.

Time and space are physically immutable. It is surprising to me that this simple fact seems to elude us, or at least I have not seen it explained as such.

Even more surprising to me is that we have not harnessed continuous motion with the natural forces in the universe as we know them. I do not call it *perpetual motion*, since all mechanical matter decomposes (wears out) and replacement is necessary, so *perpetual* is somewhat of a misrepresentation technically. But continuous motion seems to be a reality that I have several ways I could explain to make this possible without fossil or other material fuels. Yet I never see much on the subject other than "it cannot be done because it violates a thermodynamic theorem." I would note that if our theorems are based on the logic that matter is time and therefore time slows down, then I rest my case.

Please also see this article, where the second law of thermodynamics is challenged: http://www.scientificamerican.com/article.cfm?id=how-nature-breaks-the-second-law from Scientific American Magazine. This article further supports my premise regarding energy and its continuous potential.

In the next section, "Smart Energy Now," I have partially detailed how to provide for continuous motion; I would like to work with someone in this field. I, of course, hope you find my explanations above of merit, so that I might find someone with mathematical background, which I certainly lack, to work with me on this project.

Section 3

Smart Energy Now

Natural forces in nature provide multiple endless energy models without expending fossil fuels. Is anyone willing to work with me who has a physics background?

What will it accomplish?

It will accomplish evolution on a monumental scale; it will accomplish migrating from a fossil-fuel world to an automated world devoid of expending fossil fuels. It will overnight, in unbounded terms, provide universal energy to the entire world, not just the industrialized nations or emerging nations. It will provide a unifying playing field for the people of all nations to find more common options in which to better communicate and improve our common understanding and standard of living.

Note: I believe these ideas sound as if I have a large dose of megalomania lodged into my gray matter, but they simply need to be tested and moved forward. Even if I am only 1 to 99 percent correct, it could change energy production as we currently understand it today.

Why is it important?

It is important

- to improve life, to advance conservation of precious fossil fuels for other uses; to change the world and provide it with greater possibilities;
- to liberate; and
- to dramatically control carbon emissions from the planet, coupled with enabling universal energy to all individuals or societies who either require or desire it.

What are the anticipated outcomes?

The outcomes would be virtually near-free recycled energy and/or regenerated energy, provided by the current clean and robust elements of energy, such as gravity, electrostatics, and magnetism—and all that implies.

What will be its enduring impact?

This project would forever alter the social structures and thereby the social requirements of the world. In other words, energy provided on an equal playing field for all people will, in effect, tie us all closer together in function and in equal choices. It would theoretically replace monopolies and cartels with freedom, as well as being groundbreaking for all of physics and all sciences in general.

Further project description

This project began with me as a child trying to figure out how to automatically run my tricycle and my little green army jeep, which required peddling a wheel or armature bar to turn the wheels. I was obviously a lazy kid who did not desire to labor too much to pedal through the sidewalks and streets in my youthful days! I remember constructing the concept using magnets, and then let the idea fade as I entered school and grew up as a young man going to school and then on to my working career. Just before I retired, I was still intrigued by the idea, and began to construct the project in my garage, with some success. However, I soon realized I needed a physics partner with a background in electronics, especially electrostatics and the mathematics to aid in the assumptions as well as scribe in the language of science the calculated results. I knew that would take some higher levels of mathematical language, certainly beyond my expertise.

Once these multiple ideas of automatic energy, which I mused about in my youth, are detailed, I will give away the intellectual property to anyone with a hint of conceptual capability. I am very willing to give the intellectual property away, but I would like to work on the project.

In simple terms, you may think it violates the fundamental thermodynamic entropy theology that we have all been indoctrinated with. By the way, I consider thermodynamic science more a theology and manifest scotoma in our lexicon, rather than a fact. In my own humble opinion, physics is incalculable, and to rely on definitions is to limit physics or existence itself. Neither have limits; therefore—in my puny assumptive world—physics is forever a living definition, as well as a fixed proof, much as infinity is both sides of the same coin at once.

Therefore, I will fundamentally argue that thermodynamic entropy is relative for like-for-like kinetic actions, which will diminish force, as it today properly outlines.

However, if you change the like-for-like concepts when generating energy, you change the rules by which thermodynamic entropy was developed. In other words, if you use two dimensions to generate kinetic energy, complemented in equal response to one dimension generating its own energy, you alter or augment the output energy produces. Hence, the like-for-like action = reaction is modified, and the results are not like for like. Action can multiply reaction. This provides for a gear ratio that augments energy output using natural forces, as well as other forces (fossil fuels too.)

This process uses natural forces, such as electrostatics, magnetism, and gravity, among other natural stores of energy, in a form that is non-relative, or in other words, uses a differential gear ratio that trumps lost energy. It does so by way of leveraging opposite dimensions and gravity. Thus, it changes the scientific or theological rules that constricted the methods used to define generic thermodynamics. In other words, thermodynamics becomes truly dynamic, rather than static.

Formulas: (See definitions in **Bold** below.)

1. Electrostatics created by D^2 + G in Linear 1D = CM
2. M+ (+ &—) + G = CM * *Note:* Electrostatics could be included to augment output.
3. Combination of both formulas to leverage ultimate energy output potential.

D = Dimensions; G = Gravity; CM = Continuous Motion; E= Electrostatics; 1D = 1 Dimension

Simply stated: It combines linear and non-linear actions to produce energy that is continuous.

Note: There are two basic methods: 1. G&E (gravity and electrostatics), and 2. M+G (magnetism and gravity).

Stated in another fashion, there are two possible methods: 1) independent of electrostatics, which uses gravity and magnetism); and 2) with the use of electrostatics in combined ways to achieve natural energy from natural forces:

1. This form uses dimensions x 2 (down and side to side) run by gravity (non-linear), generating electrostatics combined with a linear (up) dimension. This linear and non-linear interaction provides the mechanisms to create a gear ratio that multiplies

itself. Hence, you gain continuous motion, which could then provide for heat and other outputs to generate endless energy.

2. This form uses both positive and negative magnetism in graduated powers to direct motion in an upward direction opposing gravity, and then uses electrostatics captured in the downward thrust to leverage additional energy, which is then redeployed again and again by magnetism alone in an upward motion. *Note:* The electromagnetism is not necessary, but a natural benefit that should be leveraged from the simple process of motion (which both gravity and motion provide for).

   Variations of these forms of operations are dependent on mechanical engineering.

- Additionally, electrostatics can be enhanced by using a circular glass ball, for instance, with other internal triboelectric materials to augment the energy produced beyond the direct gravity effects of triboelectric stimulus, using for example, a Teflon tube and a glass ball. These two materials, glass and Teflon, are near opposites for electron transfer on the triboelectric scale, which generates electrostatics. The electrostatics would be captured within a capacitor for electric generation.

Note: I use the term *continuous motion* versus *perpetual motion*, since all mechanical matter decomposes (wears out). Perpetual is generally an accurate statement, except for matter decay, for at that point, motion ceases.

Thermodynamics fundamentally proposes that you cannot squeeze blood from a turnip. Or in other words, energy depletes and will not sustain itself. But if you change the mechanical genetics of the turnip, you can. Metaphorically and practically that can be accomplished when energy and matter are merged together in a completely clean and virtually innocuous manner. You simply apply three-dimensional forces in a manner that leverages two dimensions against or in complement to one dimension. It's nature working at its best. it's that simple.

With the continuous motion of matter, then heat or additional motion receptors can be activated, generating excess energy, superseding the level of energy required to generate this continuous motion of matter. Thus, continuous energy is produced by way of natural forces—gravity, magnetism, and electrostatics. it sounds highly improbable given current thinking, but intellectually it is quite plausible. Again, my goal is to work with a lab of scientists to pursue this objective, as I have outlined above. It may seem obscure, but once I share the simple mechanics of this idea, I hope you will find it of interest and most importantly possible. If it is possible, the world changes. I know it sounds in large part to be more than just a bit delusional, but even if we leverage 50 percent of this potential, we succeed beyond what exists today and provide for the clean and necessary energy the world depends upon.

Ultimate objectives and gains:

Secondarily this project, if actualized, would, I believe, secure the highest accolades worldwide due to its unique utilization of continuous motion and would therefore support the investment returns to the philanthropists and scientists involved. Foremost it will be humanity changing for the good, providing a leap in the advance of science and living standards for the people of this world. It will expedite the integration of humanity by tying us together via sources of energy necessary to improve communication and common living standards that would better integrate the world, coupled with the saving of fossil fuels for other uses, combined with less pollution. In that process, it would hopefully improve understanding and common cause among us all, rather than living with the continuing social divides that hinder those decent objectives.

In sharing these thoughts on the potentials for energy production with new methodologies, it is my objective to find someone seriously interested to pursue these ideas.

Simply and profoundly, that is my end goal.

These concepts are actually basic, and the mechanics I have in mind to build a working model would not be difficult given access to scientists in the area of physics and electrostatics, along with some very common materials.

Summary

We exist because of the concept called a paradox. Paradoxes have no answers; they can never be broken. They are the infinite fuel of existence itself.

These ideas I have shared have been a growing process, so they will seem somewhat contradictory or paradoxical at times, but at a basic level, they seek the same objective of simplifying perceptions, based as much on common sense as on our ever-evolving science. The quantum world is truly our birthplace, so it holds our commonality, but as its fundamental structure builds the matter we exist with and by, it may morph its fundamentals in the process. Simply, I believe that to begin our scientific pursuits, we do best when we can start at the beginning with a common foundation and with practical principles, which give rise to a better result in our end conclusions as we pursue the Holy Grail of knowledge.

My hope is that those of you who disagree or find value with my points of thought will augment this discussion and we will, in the end, all move forward.

Final thought

The quantum world is the sole genesis of all we are, combined with the infinite realm, which I believe bares the inscrutable nature of space and time, whether we as sentient philosophical beings exist or not.

In my worldview, if a tree falls and no one's there to hear it, it still makes a sound.

Infinity and evolution survive us all—forever! But in the interim of our existence, this ebb and flow throughout time, I believe, enhances knowledge. Therefore, with the growth of true knowledge, we will improve the betterment of how we treat one another. Consequently, science is the basis for all truth; hence, it is either the practical or metaphorical face of God, if you believe in such things, as science underpins philosophy's truths and failures, as well.

Therefore, science is a worthy journey indeed.

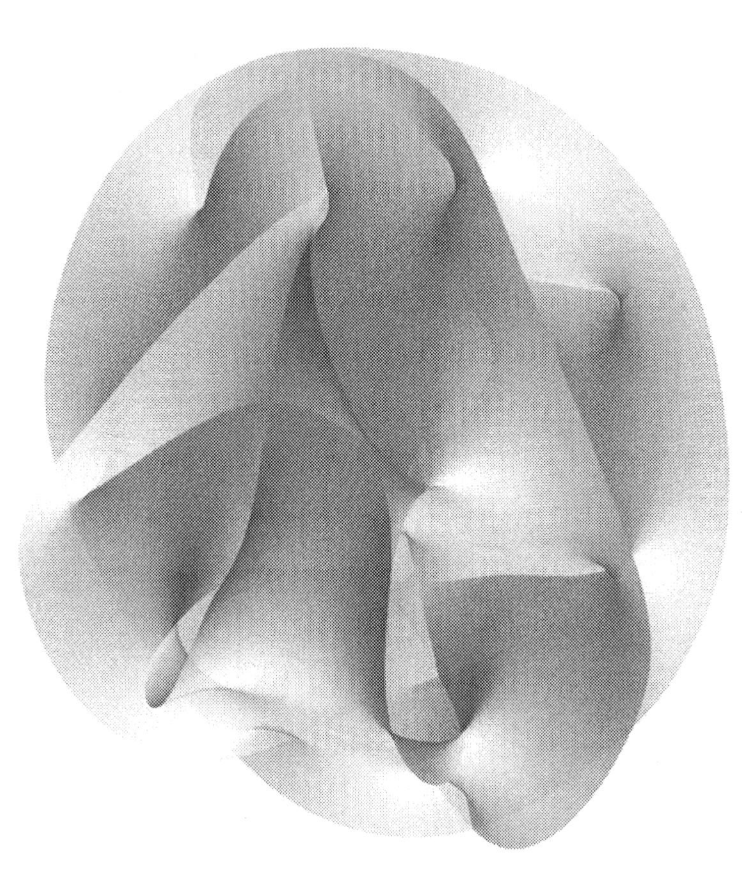

Chapter 31

WHAT IS EXISTENCE?

From wonder into wonder, existence opens.
—Lao Tzu

Well, get in line. This question seems to trump everyone when we try to grasp what actually is beyond our reach. Keep in mind that we are finite sentient beings, with a limited capability to understand everything. Did not the so-called God in the Judeo-Christian Bible state in replete terms that to try to understand him was futile and beyond our ability? If you are a person of ideological faith, you would be wise to take note.

If you believe you can understand existence through faith, superstition, mythology, mathematics, or the physics of relativity, space-time, momentum space, quantum or phase space, string theory, or just by simply unifying the four known forces, again, get in line, one in which you will contribute to the discussion and produce some often positive results, but will miss asking the right question. And that question is fundamental to understanding, to truth, to ad-infinitum fact. You will never as a finite being or even an infinite being, if such a thing were possible, have the capability to understand this question: "What is existence?" beyond the intuitive knowledge that you will never know, except for your common sense that it is real, just as you experience pain and joy. It is that simple.

To review all of the models that attempt to assume they may find the theory of everything is a pondering that will bear fruit, just as a whittler improves at his craft through the years, but the whittler will never reach perfection. The fruit, the beauty of the rainbow, not the end pot of gold, is the true gold or reward that will improve our lives, balanced with a single guideline as we forever scientifically discover, and that guideline is the Golden Rule.

Unify these elements of knowledge and the Golden Rule, and we will treat ourselves and others better, far beyond any leader's, potentate's, or politician's wanting chatter.

And by the way, this should raise an eyebrow or two: the four known forces are already unified. Yet we have missed the core of that issue: gravity's variability, or the relative nature of gravity. Once this is more fully understood, the four forces will be unified on paper, but it will not change our understanding of the universe or of our existence. Unity or unification of existence must be combining the infinite with the finite, and that is, as I have said for years, a twain that shall never meet. They will coexist as they must to provide the balance to existence itself, but they are as separate as separate can be. One is limited, and one is omniscient. One has an alpha and an omega, and one has no alpha or omega. One is comprehensible, and one is forever non-comprehensible.

If you were able to transcend from the finite to the infinite, you would no longer have knowledge, ego, hope, joy, pain, or suffering, as these are all based on definitions that have limits, and the infinite has no limits. In fact, the infinite may be all of the things I have mentioned, but you would never have the awareness to know it, as that would define you as an entity, and to be an entity would make you by definition finite. This conundrum, this paradox, is the power of existence and its reality, which will defy all attempts to define existence, as once defined, it hence becomes finite. That is a thought equation that will never be trumped.

So the quest for the theory of everything, while I consider it critical and essential to better our everyday finite life, is not a realistic prize that has an end. It is a prize only for those who are committed to the journey and what that journey produces for all of us along the way.

So I say, "Here, here!" to knowledge, as knowledge has unlocked the world from many a mythological torment and brought us forward into the honest fruits of our minds' better natures and to a better life and into the light of truth.

Just because we must acknowledge many fragmented and misguided efforts in our experience to learn, we only better ourselves through humility in that process, coupled with the knowledge gained, as our commitment is strengthened as the fabric of the truly caring and strength of character is born as we continue to whittle away. To give up on the pursuit of knowledge is to give up on goodness; it is to give up on what some might call a god. I harbor no ill will to the motivations of knowledge, as long as they are balanced with that single issue I raised before, the Golden Rule.

Please never give up. For once we do, we give in and let the tyrants of truth and the ideologues of ancient times, who selfishly ran the world, rear their heads again. That is where we came from, and shame on anyone not willing to introspectively move forward—always—and put the attributes and attitudes of children behind us, as now we are adults and should behave as such.

Today we see a resurgence of such ideological faith-based neophytes detracting us away from knowledge, causing heinous harm to themselves and others by blowing themselves up in the name of Allah or God for a cause or causes for which all rationality is lost and completely devoid of the Golden Rule. We must through knowledge and the unity that technology can manifest put an end to this horror. No government, individual, religion, or culture should be allowed to trump the Golden Rule and the intrinsic nature of goodness for their culture. If they do, they should be institutionalized to protect the rest of the world from misguided horror and harm. This should be a global principle to protect the unprotected.

Just imagine if someday these so-called ideological vultures who prey on the poor and ignorant to do their evil deeds were met by people with an education, who had the advanced science that provided universal energy to run their homes and shelters. I daresay these vultures would meet a more unified and decent world, with greater equality and means to defeat these demagogues of truth. Education and technology would unite those heretofore impoverished in spirit and purpose and provide a decent means of living to unify with others more fairly, and they would limit the power of selfish leaders. Knowledge, education, and technology on a ubiquitous level will change this world. It will not be done with guns, bombs, or politicians. It will be done with science and the practical caring for others. And, I will say it again, with the Golden Rule, which is at the core of nearly all religions, but has been manipulated by many selfish clergy, monks, and mullahs. This is the world we are in today; we are today so advanced and mature from our cruel past, and yet still so selfish and corrupt in so many parts of the world. Science can stop this cruelty. To that end, I am going to suggest some hope for the future through the improvement of science as I continue the review of what existence is.

It is critical to note that the four known forces (electromagnetic, gravity, weak, strong) seem to drive so much conversation and interest, as the missing link has appeared to be quantum gravity. However, take it from me! I disagree, as I have already stated—big surprise. Let me explain why one more time. In brief:

Gravity is variable or relative, even though it is considered the weakest of all the four forces. In other words, at the quantum level, it is supremely weak and possibly impacted as well by the force of quarks, protons, electrons, dark energy, and dark matter, and the list goes on. Given its extreme weakness, it is superseded by other forces at work.

However, move gravity to the arena of a black hole, and it currently, from what we understand today, supersedes every other force. It is so strong not even a photon or light can theoretically escape.

In summary: due to the variability of the strength of gravity based on its environment, it is unified with the other three forces.

Fundamental as well is the point I have already made about the infinite and the finite above. We need to grasp this central issue to understand that the term unification is a vagary, as some things will be unified and other things will simply not be. There are knowns, and there are forever going to be unknowns. To assume beyond this premise wastes mental energy.

Now, to close this essay on what existence is, as I have said, the pursuit of knowledge is at the core of changing our existence for the better. So I would like to end with a subject based on that issue. This relates to "Smart Energy Now," which I have written about in section 3 of chapter 30. But I am going to reiterate it to be reviewed again in chapter 30.

Energy in common, combined with knowledge, will change the world. Then we will change existence itself for the better.

Chapter 32

Everything Is Nothing, and Nothing Is Everything

Nothingness does not denote a lack of importance; it denotes humility, and hence everything.

Provocative; perhaps weird and illogical—yes indeed. But that is the paradox, the conundrum that fits into the open box of ideas and ultimate logic as we ponder the nature of existence, which has no beginning and no end.

To begin this story, I need to address some fundamentals, with a few leaps from the intuitive aspects of our minds. That story begins with the physics we live within and how it operates or, at a minimum, what we currently understand, which is not the whole story, to be certain. As the whole story involves infinity, which must defy understanding, except for our ever-evolving quest for knowledge, it will always come up wanting, as infinity, by definition, is beyond complete comprehension.

As you will hear me repeat over and over again and again, if infinity were comprehensible, it would have limits and therefore defy its own nature, that is, become finite. It would be a mere fairy tale of our mental illusions. And truth is not an illusion. So make no mistake about the limits of your comprehension. They exist and will forever exist, except for impressions found through instinctive logic, or perhaps better said, instinctive illogic, but not from any firm notion through the pining and persistent efforts of mathematical truths, which are finite at best.

To begin this story, I will begin discussing some premises of physics, beginning with quantum mechanics, from which we all are born. Quantum physics seems in some sense to be the bridge between the infinite and the finite, but that is just a definition formed from the limits that words hold us to. In truth, I believe the finite and the infinite are absolutes that never meet, except with some exceptions by way of the quantum world, which contains the weird science that mirrors both worlds through entanglement and superpositions, among other obscure physical realities that defy explanation in either a finite or infinite form of definition.

Note: This bridge that quantum mechanics provides is a window into two existences, from which the mechanics actually allow life itself, as well as infinity, to exist or coexist with the finite. One is not possible without the other.

Unlike classical physics, which simply tells us that 2 + 2 = 4, quantum physics is the source or bearer of our birth as sentient beings. Without the weirdness and mystery of the quantum, we would dangle in despair, trying to elucidate or impose the classical model of life as the core of physics. And the classical model it is not, except for the world of the finite, the whole core of physics. Our classical mathematics proves clearly that its own mathematics and science will never resolve the answer to infinity. Infinities are the possible province only of the quantum and of the infinite. For us as finite sentient beings, these obscurities that trump mathematical formulas to understand will do so and be so forever—or at the very least, preach of an agnostic truth, which will be all that is left to human sciences, save for perceptions perhaps.

To clarify, the alpha and the omega have no beginning and no end. To suggest otherwise would be to live in a fairy tale, which we often do to find answers, when we should actually admit to our ideological selves and rather commit to reality as it spells itself out, with answers and non-answers.

After all, these are just the simple facts of the finite existence we occupy, as consciousness is a confined term. If we were infinite, or omniscient, we would not be conscious, as that would limit us. Again, this may seem to be a foggy concept, but it is really very basic and important to understand. I will continue to repeat and hound upon this premise while I explain the fundamentals of existence as they exist, regardless of my point of view.

A brief explanation

Note: Quantum and classical physics have never fully resolved themselves with similar physics, yet both exist. The classical world is made of objects we can see and touch, such as plastic, metal, humans, animals, and stars, as well as conceptually space and time. The quantum world is made of micro-particles, such as atoms, electrons, photons, quarks, neutrinos, and the list goes on. But these micro-particles make up the macro-particles of us: human beings, cars, dirt, asphalt, and the matter we see and touch. To briefly touch on this subject and the objective distinctions, I will give you a couple of examples. If in our macro-world (finite matter), I throw a baseball at two windows on a wall, it will only go through one of the windows, but in the micro-world of the quantum particle world, if I throw an electron or a photon at that same window, it will go through both windows at the same time. Logically it makes no sense, but it has been proven by experiment. Additionally we have a premise in the quantum mechanical world called entanglement: it defies the speed of light and treats all objects as if they were local to one another, rather than separate. In other words, if I had two micro-particles, such as a photon, millions of miles apart, and I changed the spin of one companion particle photon, its counterpart millions of miles away would change its spin at the very same time. This has also been experimentally proven. But logically in a classical physics world, this does not happen, as we are bound by the laws of the speed of light, or what is known as local and non-local behavior.

Even beyond the quantum science we are now observing from within our finite world, quantum mechanics still defies complete explanation. It is a reality we will never fully know, as it is uncaged by infinity itself. I would suggest that the quantum world is the link between a twain that will never meet: the infinite and the finite, yet they coexist through our necessary quantum partnership.

To reiterate: in fact, if the truth be known, everything is nothing and nothing is everything, thanks to the quantum, which gives us our very lives as sentient beings, as it is from quantum particles that we form matter in the form of our finite selves. Beyond that province of sentiency, we are captives of a mystery, forever unresolved but not unacknowledged.

Infinity is and will forever be of a weirdness to the classical mind, as the mind itself is finite, yet quantum truth is outside that circumscribed realm, and hence it is additionally of infinite bias, even though some physicists will assert that quantum physics works within the classical physics and mathematics of our finite world, and I will agree in degrees at a molecular level, it appears to have some credence.

In this reality or our own macro-based matter, interdependence emerges that makes it possible for our classical world of physics to even exist, coupled with the quantum, from which we are born. The classical world is not inevitable, but plausible, given time, which actually does not exist, or more appropriately exists within a superposition within the quantum world. Now figure that one out. However, you will never really know, other than to possibly gaze at the truth of a logic not seemingly possible.

But do not even try, other than in a quasi-reality of inquisitiveness, as infinite reality is beyond our finite sentient minds. Infinity cannot and will not be defined. To make it so would violate its very nature in an uncircumspect manner, as the very definition of infinity is something beyond our finite comprehension.

If it were comprehensible, it would therefore be circumscribed, that is, defined. Infinity, by implicit definition, is not defined. It is omniscient. If it were understandable, it would be defined, hence circumscribed, and therefore no longer infinite.

It is a conundrum that haunts the obscure ends of knowledge and confines us to live in an unknown, not-fully defined existence, as well as encourages us to pursue knowledge forever. To not pursue knowledge would be to withdraw from life itself—or at least a full and productive life that has the potential through knowledge to build bridges, that brings us together in more common terms, rather than live in the divides we exist in today, albeit those divides were even worse in times of ancient pasts. Just review your history and the beliefs of many saints and sinners that slavery, concubines, caste systems, and the torture of witches and infidels were of goodness and right; today the majority of the world would argue the opposite. Our history and technological advances have given us a much better assessment of the cultures that have gone before us, and we are improving for the most part I would hope.

One of the greatest thought problems or thought equations is similarly based on the concept of a God or an omniscient deity that is based on faith, not reality, as most theologians and scholars would agree [1]. Today it still is causing great hardships and divides between peoples, when theoretically religion should be bringing us together, if one believes in the goodness of such religions and theoretically humane philosophies.

I will describe such an ancient thought problem and solution, hence thought equation, below; however, the solution within our current multicultural reality will be abridged by those who believe in ideological faith and culture versus fact as their truth.

Thought equations: Sentient beings are finite and for the sake of argument coexist inside the infinite. In other words, finite life is not omniscient, but infinity is so, just as a possible God is described as such, however correctly or erroneously. *Note:* I hope this thought equation will define that answer for you, even if the correctness of the answer fundamentally proves to be agnostic.

If we can agree that finite things are only possible within an infinite (omniscient) existence, as infinity encompasses the finite world we all live within, then the following thought equation holds true; otherwise we would be of a duality, both finite and infinite. There is no mathematics or logic that would hold to a finite object being infinite. It is simply not possible. Finite and infinite definitions are implicitly not the same, as finite is finite and infinite is infinite. Never will that twain meet. One is limited, and one is not.

A very simple logical proof

1. The proof in the paragraph above is an absolute that cannot violate itself.
2. Infinity, by definition, has no center point, is boundless, and has no beginning and no end; hence, it will never be understood by a sentient mind by way of philosophy or mathematics, which hail from the finite world we all live within together. This proof is sacrosanct, as finite mathematics breaks down and fails when describing the infinite. *Note:* Ask any mathematics major if infinities are solvable.
3. I want to also note that within an infinite existence, there can be no love, no joy, no pain, no knowledge, no ego. To apply any attribute to the infinite is to limit it and define it. That which cannot be understood, such as infinity, cannot be defined in our conventional terms, such as a = a. Again, such provinces of mathematics and philosophy exist solely to the finite species.
4. Infinity is actually impossible to comprehend. Logically it is impossible, yet we know it is. For instance, the notion of no alpha and no omega, no beginning and no end—how does that make any logical sense? However, the inverse of that

illogic is the finite, which grows and lives by way of hopeful logic, along with selfishness and illogic as well. But the decent goal for sentient beings is the Golden Rule and the growth of knowledge to better humanity's health and caring. But I do digress somewhat here. My primary point is that logic keeps on track based on our finite existence, not based on our infinite notions of deities, which would be by definition circumscribing God or infinity and the omniscient to a thing, or finite object. Infinity will not be tamed with such wishful illusions [2].

5. In summary, the finite may transition to the infinite or the infinite to the finite, but they will never and can never meet. Just to repeat myself, just do the math, or ask any mathematician if infinities can be defined. In a word, no, they cannot. So we only can inject faith to find a god or gods, and we will never and can never know the truth of such a question, in point of fact. It is a fickle life we lead, quite radically and factually.

So what does this mean regarding classical and quantum physics? It means too often we know less than we think we do. Myself included! Yet theoretical physicists and cosmologists, among other philosophers and pursuers of truth, are rubbing upon the wisps of truth that we are not all we seem to be, and even more. They are doing this by the measures of science, coupled with intuitive perceptions, which would have been unthinkable just a century ago. In fact, they would have been the Copernicuses and Galileos in another time, which would have had them killed for such heretical, non-cultural thinking; they were opposing truths believed to be ideologically sacrosanct in times past.

We are on the verge of a highly valued knowledge not bound by ideology or faith, but brought about largely by science, which is peeling away, not only at legacies, which some hold as inviolable building blocks, but at the legacies of its own science. We are reaching to a vision of scientific weirdness, possibly hard to swallow, yet possibly of fact more than fiction. Clearly we may never know, as this journey is peering into the relationship of the infinite, the quantum, and our home foundations are built upon the finite from the highest levels of sentiency. It is a coexistent venture to examine the possible with the so-called impossible, or the finite with the infinite; that is where we are headed. The results may reveal those bridges that I spoke of to mend past wrongs and improve our daily lives, not for just some, but for all. It is a lofty notion, but a result that lays in wait as the knowledge of science and philosophy of this world improves.

In 1935 Erwin Schrödinger came up with a thought experiment whereby the micro—and macro-worlds collided. His seemingly logical supposition was that a micro-world radioactive atom could both decay and not decay at the same time if linked to a bottle of cat poison, based on superpositions' dual state proven in quantum physics. Therefore a macro-world cat could be either dead or alive, all dependent upon the mere observation of a human opening up a cage and looking at the cat.

Hence, everything is nothing and nothing is everything, if you will. However, I have often found this premise of a micro-world (atom) and a macro-world (cat) superposition state as not being accurate—which would negate my own thesis. Although it holds an interest, or novelty at any rate, for me, it is not the sacrosanct proof I find compelling.

Vlatko Vedral, a professional physicist, has entertained the notion that the quantum world also works in union far more than we realize with the macro-world. Please read his very substantial and intriguing article in *Scientific American* [3]. I believe that Vlatko Vedral is glimpsing the true realm of physics as it will progress. He touches on the known and unknown as equals in my view. And this is where real physics of the future is headed.

I also want to note an article from *New Science* by Anil Ananthaswamy, who points out other experiments and rationales regarding the distinctions between the quantum and the classical physics worlds [4].

The sum total of these articles rubs up against the very nature of existence, which is not definable by my belief system or by logic in my view; they are grasping at the core of an open physics system that may open our philosophical gazes to new hopes and heights.

In summary, we are living in a system that is for all practical purposes of our lives both local and non-local, except for infinity, which may debunk every known mathematical formula ever devised, thus bringing a balance to the chaos of entropy and allow for both infinity and the finite to exist as disparate and as equals at the same time.

To answer the question what is reality. Coexistence of the finite and infinite, hence complete abstraction and scientific proofs posits balance as the only final answer. To propose otherwise would explode and dismantle the logic of an educated mind to extinction, as it grasps the impossible nature of no beginning and no end and allows for life within a closed environment that sees no farther than the logic of the self within bounds we hold as true, even if they are not.

In truth, what I mean for most of us is that we will never have the misfortune to engage endless infinities of reality within our own minds. If our minds were caught in endless infinite loops, as mathematical definitions of infinity are, the experience of that truth in such educated detail would mentally cause a compulsive, unrelenting phobia. That truth is the experience of infinity or the thought-provoking notion of the essence of endlessness. Such an awareness would negate purpose and the necessity of a conclusion or ultimate answers to be sought. In poignant truth, such an end conclusion will never be found. Therefore, the mind may only dismay itself to pain and demise in that perfect view of nature's full experience. Therefore, the climb to knowledge, not final conclusions, is a noble and good purpose. It is the rainbow's trail that is the gold, not the end destination!

Today most of us only experience the notions of black and white, of yes and no, of a wrong and a right. But the truth of life is that these notions are found more truly in the gray areas of life, in the mix of realities, the truth that entropy is part of some realities such as the finite but not the infinite, that quantum physics within the areas of entanglement and superpositions defies common sense and finite definitions—coupled with other intuitive queries into subjects such as time may have other dimensions, along with multiverses. All of these queries into the plausible are not beyond the intuitive nature of thought, but many may well be beyond the mathematical proofs or enormous energies required to prove [5]. Simply food for thought: thermodynamic violation of its second law.

In other words, existence/life is in balance, even as entropy wildly abounds via its finite roots, coupled by way of its nonexistence through the infinite nature of existence, which no one can explain. *Note:* Here is a riddle for the ages: do all things, through the ebb and flow of existence, exist and not—exist?

Actually, everything is nothing and nothing is everything gives us logic and life/existence via balance. In other words, there is time, and there is no time; there is space, and there is no space; everything is connected, and yet is separate—certainly given entanglement, superpositions, and the infinite, which supersede any hope for understanding. These conundrums reinforce a science fundamentally raw and necessarily incomprehensible, which gives rise to the firm and balanced mechanics of existence in general. Make no mistake: it is a violent and turbulent universe we are engaged in at this point of our existences, but that is nature in symphonic rage and glory—yet I believe it exists as a result of perfect balance out of a realm of nature without an alpha or omega. That premise is essential, and yet incomprehensible. The virtue of that irony is that it gives us nature, as it always has been and always will be. If we understood it, the balance would be gone, and that I find impossible.

Note: That balance is no respecter of humanity [6].A wise human biblical reference—"God is no respecter of persons"—or its often violent and harsh human torments, it is only a respecter of lifes own nature. We, living within the finite, must take on the horror of nature's and humankind's tragedies alone and together. Therefore, it is fundamental to put away youthful visions, imaginations, superstitions, and mythologies as such of the ancients, whose knowledge was of a child's knowledge based on our science of today.

To quote a wise biblical human-made phrase: "When I was a child, I spoke as a child, I understood as a child, I thought as a child: but when I became a man, I put away childish things" (1 Cor. 13:4). We should take heed.

The novel and interesting potential fallout of the relatively empty endless abyss we exist within has no logical answer; if you programmed computers that were as large as a solar system, they would literally burn themselves out into failure as the circuit boards burned out at the impossible task of understanding infinity. Some of us as humans have glimpsed the ultimate jail and inevitability of existence, and it too can cause a suffocating mental breakdown for some people sometimes, at least for me on occasion. My point is that if we are truly honest and fully focused, our minds would break down if we ever fully looped onto the endlessness and seeming pointlessness of existence. My only relief is to imagine an ebb and flow of existence, which fully dies as we know it and is reborn again and again, and then the hopelessness of no end seems ironically less confining. Without conclusion, what is the point of anything? That is a riddle I have been challenged with for a lifetime.

That is the only way it can be if we are a part of existence in either a finite or impossible infinite form, as there is no twain, even via quantum mechanics' illumination of its potential mysteries, that will ever combine both finite knowledge and the infinite as a sentient or otherwise type of conscious thought or equation.

The sentient search is essential to improve on life, and it's inevitable—forever—as I logically believe sentiency will come and go, as time, multidimensional or not, also will come and go in a relative manner, if you choose to believe so. Still, for us as sentient beings and objects of matter, we are finite, and for me if a tree falls and no one hears it, it still makes a sound. Time and space are immutable to the conscious mind, even if time and space are of a bizarre nature that really does not exist—in some form of entanglement, for example. I believe infinity connects us all. Quite the story, this existence we are engaged in.

The big picture, or grand reality beyond our mere selves, is and will be a riddle, an enigma, a paradox, a conundrum, undisposed of forever.

Simply said, with the only means available through a poetic depth, we are in balance, by being both local and non-local, by existing via the only describable manner possible: we are and we are not. Everything is nothing, and nothing is everything—*period*. We live in the perfection of balance, which will never find any other description except illusion.

However, the pursuit of knowledge from our roots (the quantum, intuition, and science per se) is a humble and humane effort. This exciting, noble, and extraordinary pursuit of knowledge must trump all obstacles. In doing so, it will, if we follow the Golden Rule, find our commonality as a species and all species, and as a result, better our health, lives, and understanding through the diminution of torment and harm that a world of a misguided historic diversity has only seemed to continue with its useless egos and destruction.

Knowledge is power, and power is curative. So goes the balance I look for in life and the understanding that we are all one, from dust to dust, in the end. We are different in our randomness and the same in such. A simple paradox of life.

References:

[1] "For no one may see me and live" (Exod. 33:20, referring to God). This illustrates some ancient and wise individuals, who understood the divide between the infinite (omniscient/God, if you will) and the finite.
[2] Ibid.
[3] Vlatko Vedral, "Living in a Quantum World," *Scientific American*, June 2011, 38, 43.
[4] Anil Ananthaswamy, "Quantum Reality Is What You Make It," *New Science*, June 2011, 13.
[5] J. Miguel Rubin, "The Long Arm of the Second Law," *Scientific American*, October 2008, 63–67.

[*] Russ Otter, "Is Reality Digital or Analog?" FQXi Community, February 2011. http://fqxi.org/data/essay-contest-files/Otter_Our_Universe_Digital_1.pdf. Also see chapter 30, "Our Universe, Science, and Potentials in Review."

[6] Biblical references in several places: Genesis 4:4, 5; Acts 10:34, 35; Romans 2:9–11; among many others within the Judeo-Christian Bible.

Chapter 33

CONNECTIONS

The cycle of life—it's an implicit paradox. Enjoy the journey.

The binding of existence is a story built upon knowledge, intuition, and speculation. In the end, it is built upon some known theoretically successfully tested truths and some unknowns conveyed in a formula that I consider trumps any objections as we ponder the scope of existence. First, we know of existence by way of our self-awareness, coupled with scientific knowledge. Second, we know of existence by way of the unknowns, that is, infinity, which must incongruously play with us (self-aware, finite creatures) in some connected manner.

This second, irascibly indefinable thing called infinity simply stumps our finite minds every time when we attempt to figure out its mathematical infinities—as it must. If it did not stump our efforts to understand it, it would become defined, and anything defined is finite. So we have an absolute conundrum that operates our existence. But we are still connected, in a union, both finite and infinite, through the known attributes we have scientifically tested to be true. Without infinity, there can be no finite. And remember, infinity has no bounds, no time limits, no space limits, no beginning and no end.

This is plainly contrary to finite logic, but infinity simply is contrary. It always has been, and it always will be. But it is also the very milk of our very finite existences. We are connected. Our actions matter, as I will soon explain in the summary.

Infinity: irascible and fundamentally a necessary fickle fact. An argument that no mathematics or thought equation can defend against. To challenge this premise is to supersede infinity's very nature. It will never, ever happen.

Therefore, we are circumscribed to live within physics largely of Newtonian and Einstein's mathematics. I would caution that these finite mathematics are subject to change. They currently work fairly well for our finite existence as we mathematically calculate how to penetrate and maneuver the stars or add 2 plus 2 to equal 4. But they do not work to unravel quantum mechanics (in total) and the cache of oddities, such as superpositions, whereby subatomic particles are in several places at one time until they are interrupted by measurement. Nor do these current finite mathematics explain entanglement, which allows for two subatomic elements or even molecules to be millions of miles apart; however, if one changes its state of spin or electrical charge, the other particle millions of miles away responds instantly. Yes, this violates the concept of the speed of light as the fastest method of action in the universe.

Einstein called entanglement spooky but nonetheless real. Entanglement seemingly violates the speed of light. But hold on: while the speed of light travels, entanglement implies connection or lack of the necessity to travel, what is known as local action versus action at a distance. The rules of cause and effect become defunct from all convention when entanglement is at play.

Space is the key to this thought equation. Since space is infinite to the finite observer, space in this context is also in union with waves, as well as particles. However, waves may connect all things instantly, just as waves may allow for superpositions.

The answer is simply that this makes us both local and non-local at the same time. Waves and/or theoretical strings, from string theory, are perhaps in some union—connected to our space and possibly time in ways we do not fully comprehend. If true, our infinite extended connections are observed from a finite realm only. It might be important to note here that simply no distance is allowed in an infinite realm, as infinity is immune to classification, and therefore it is all things and no things at the same time. Make sense? It usually should not, as finite logic has a difficult time with these both intuitively and implicitly mathematically. Make sense yet?

Probably not, as this means that everything is nothing and nothing is everything. Hence, there are no real infinites to calculate in an infinite realm. But this last statement is a clear oxymoron, as it should be, as infinity does not have mathematics or anything defined based in or of it, as this would imply a finite realm. It is simply infinite and does not apply to our finite realm of mathematics or cognitive reason.

Mathematics is purely the purview of the finite, as is reason.

When I said there are really no infinities in the infinite realm, I meant it. But to us, within the finite realm or finite conscious state as observers, infinities are what infinity, space, and time are made of. Once again, the ultimate and infinite conundrum. However, how does this allow for the stuff of existence, such as us, or cars, trees, and so on to exist? Well, we do need infinity to have a finite realm, as I said.

That is the puzzle. That must never be answered technically, nor can it be, again from a finite perspective or finite observer. This mind trap we are caught in trying to view infinity would seem to drive one mad to think that infinity, space, and time have no beginning nor an end.

But get used to it.

Infinity is indelible. Terms like *time* and *space* are non-words to describe infinity correctly, as infinity never had a beginning or an end. The space and time word terms we use within the realm of infinity's definition, or lack thereof, could not and do not exist in the infinite world—unlike the finite world, which has an alpha and omega, dust to dust, evolution, and space to move to, and a length of time that life gives us to observe.

And that is that.

We are here by way of connections of an indefinable infinity, which has always been and will always be. Make no mistake about it. This will provide us and others forever to give sentiency a journey to discover anew—new science from physics to health, coupled with new modes of life and new cultures to come—unless an asteroid impacts the earth or a supervolcano takes us to our end of time as sentient beings. Even then, others will arise, no doubt, by way of time's infinite arrow.

The finite with a beginning and end is necessary to find hope. Just imagine living for eternity without end. That proposition would compel a person to lose goals, to have no new hopes, and actually impart a crazy madness of hopelessness. People would be in the ultimate trap, or jail, forever if self-aware. "What is the point?" one would ask oneself. And therefore, life and death are necessary.

Dust to dust, and then perhaps? Take your best shot at a faithful guess as the empirical truths are nonexistent! The options are many; the realities may be few. No one really knows. No one—save those of an ideological faith, who would argue otherwise.

Plainly beyond us, the infinite and finite will ebb and flow, and new existences will arise through an endless connection to everything for all time.

Summarizing essential points:

1. *The science is:* That Infinity is incomprehensible to any complete understanding, and the finite is limited in understanding all things, perhaps itself, and certainly infinity. The connection between the finite and the infinite operates as if everything is nothing and nothing is everything. Have fun with that analogy! As for me, it holds true, as it confirms to me that cognitive logic eventually meets the illogic of infinity. This lets us clearly know we will never actually know honestly and truthfully the answers to the great questions of life, as to know

all or truth would be to actually define a place and a time, which can only be finite. And that would defy the rules of infinity, which cannot be technically ever defined. Otherwise, it is no longer infinite; it would then become as a mere canvas with parameters. Infinity is incomprehensible—*end of story . . . yesterday, today, and tomorrow . . . in other words, forever!*

2. *The moral is:* That legacies matter. So build your legacy from one of "Goodness". The *Butterfly Effect* is always on—*and that is what really matters.*

All the best in our journeys.

Parting Thought

Life is 10 percent what happens to me and
90 percent how I react to it.
—Charles Swindoll

APPENDIX A

Though I speak with the tongues of men and of angels, and have not charity, I am become as sounding brass, or a tinkling cymbal.
And though I have the gift of prophecy, and understand all mysteries, and all knowledge; and though I have all faith, so that I could remove mountains, and have not charity, I am nothing.
And though I bestow all my goods to feed the poor, and though I give my body to be burned and have not charity, it profiteth me nothing. **(1 Cor. 13:1–3, KJV)**

Note 1: The word *charity* has been used synonymously with love in many biblical translations.

Note 2: I referred to this biblical quotation to emphasize what real faith embodies. True manifest goodness requires not only actions of goodness, but that they be done with a faith in goodness for goodness's own sake, not for personal gain. This is only possible from one's genuine faith in charity or love, as is so well described from this biblical text above.

Glossary

aether / ether. The medium supposed by the ancients to fill the upper regions of space. In physics, a hypothetical substance supposed to occupy all space.

bosons. Classification of elementary particles from quantum physics, which includes photons and many of both weak—and strong-force particles.

brane. A four-dimensional universe is restricted to a brane inside a higher-dimensional space, called the bulk. Often described as sheets/strings thinly gaged between each other, as well as integrated. Related to string theory, whereby a string is a brane, and multi-branes integrate with other dimensions or strings. If you are confused, join the club.

butterfly effect. Dependence on initial conditions in which a small change at one place can result in large differences in a later state. The name of the effect, coined by Edward Lorenz, is derived from the theoretical example of a hurricane's formation being contingent on whether or not a distant butterfly had flapped its wings several weeks earlier and started atmospheric conditions that changed the course of the future, thus creating the conditions that multiplied into a hurricane. Simply said: If I walk and mistakenly hit someone's elbow, perhaps the person being hit will move his elbow to impact hitting someone else, and thus a fight begins. Hence, a small event can impact other events in life.

entanglement. When two elementary particles, such as an electron or photon, are considered physically entangled (connected), but can be millions of miles apart. When one particle changes its state of spin or polarity, the other particle it is entangled with changes at the same moment. This is a phenomenon that supersedes the speed of light.

insidious. A plan to often entrap someone without them knowing it to do harm to them. Acting harmless, but with deceit, to create a grave effect to someone or some group.

integrity. Being whole or undivided. Personal/individual moral code. Latin derivation for individual.

leptons. A classification of weak-force elementary quantum particles, such as electrons, muons, and neutrinos.

muons. Particle physics' fundamental particle of a subatomic scale.

nascent. Emerging and/or coming into existence for the first time.

neutrino. A stable neutral elementary particle with very small or possibly zero rest mass and spin ½ that travels at the speed of light. The smallest of elementary particles, so small that billions pass through the earth without ever touching any other masses or particles, such as atoms or quarks.

pernicious. Creating *insidious* harm to someone else; evil, wicked.

pillars. A supporting column sculptured in the form of an often human figure. Columns of figures holding up floors, or, symbolically, another generation on the shoulders of another generation, each holding the next one up.

quarks. A quark is an elementary particle and a fundamental constituent of matter. Quarks combine to form composite particles called hadrons, the most stable of which are protons and neutrons, the components of atomic nuclei.

scotoma. Blind spot in someone's perception, either psychological or physiological.

sentient. Having sense perception; conscious. Self-aware.

superposition. A state in quantum physics whereby a particle can be in two states, as positive and negative, at the same time.

triboelectric. A scale of different materials that become electrically charged when they come into contact or friction with one another.